MODERN GERMANY

A Volume in the Comparative
Societies Series

OTHER TITLES IN THE COMPARATIVE SOCIETIES SERIES

Modern Japan

Harold Kerbo
California Polytechnic State University, San Luis Obispo

John A. McKinstry
California Polytechnic State University, San Luis Obispo

Modern Mexico

William Canak
Middle Tennessee State University, Murfreesboro

Laura Swanson
Middle Tennessee State University, Murfreesboro

Modern Switzerland

Aldo A. Benini
California Polytechnic State University, San Luis Obispo

Modern Iran

Grant M. Farr
Portland State University

Modern Brazil

Kevin Neuhouser
Seattle Pacific University

Modern China

Richard E. Barrett
University of Illinois at Chicago

Fang Li
University of Chicago

MODERN GERMANY

A Volume in the Comparative Societies Series

HAROLD R. KERBO
California Polytechnic State University
San Luis Obispo, California

HERMANN STRASSER
Gerhard-Mercator-Universitaet
Duisburg, Germany

Boston   Burr Ridge, IL   Dubuque, IA   Madison,WI
New York   San Francisco   St. Louis
Bangkok   Bogotá   Caracas   Lisbon   London   Madrid   Mexico City
Milan   New Delhi   Seoul   Singapore   Sydney   Taipei   Toronto

McGraw-Hill Higher Education

A Division of The McGraw-Hill Companies

MODERN GERMANY

This book is printed on acid-free paper.

1 2 3 4 5 6 7 8 9 0 FGR/FGR 9 0 9 8 7 6 5 4 3 2 1 0 9

ISBN 0-07-292819-0

Editorial director: *Phillip A. Butcher*
Sponsoring editor: *Sally Constable*
Marketing manager: *Leslie A. Kraham*
Editorial coordinator: *Kate Purcell*
Project manager: *Kimberly D. Hooker*
Production supervisor: *Michael R. McCormick*
Senior designer: *Michael Warrell*
Compositor: *Shepherd, Incorporated*
Typeface: *10/12 Palatino*
Printer: *Quebecor Printing Book Group/Fairfield*

Library of Congress Cataloging-in-Publication Data
Kerbo, Harold R.
  Modern Germany / Harold R. Kerbo, Hermann Strasser.
    p.   cm. — (Comparative societies series)
  Includes bibliographical references.
  ISBN 0-07-292819-0 (softcover)
    1. Germany—Politics and government—20th century.   2. Germany—Economic conditions—20th century.   3. Germany—Ethnic relations.   4. Germany—Social conditions—20th century.   5. National characteristics, German.   I. Strasser, Hermann, 1941–   .   II. Title.   III. Series.
  DD237.K47   2000
  943.087—dc21
                                                                                              99-21322

http://www.mhhe.com

EDITOR'S PREFACE

In one of the early scenes of the movie *Reds*, the U.S. revolutionary journalist John Reed, just back from covering the beginning of World War I, is asked by a roomful of business leaders, "What is this War really about?" John Reed stands and stops all conversation with a one-word reply—"profits." Today, war between major industrial nations would disrupt profits much more than create money for a military industrial complex. Highly integrated global markets and infrastructures support the daily life of suburban families in Chicago and urban squatter settlements in Bombay. These ties produce a social and economic ecology that transcends political and cultural boundaries.

The world is a very different place than it was for our parents and grandparents. Those rare epic events of world war certainly invaded their everyday lives and futures, but we now find that daily events thousands of miles away, in countries large and small, have a greater impact on North Americans than ever before, with the speed of this impact multiplied many times in recent decades. Our standard of living, jobs, and even prospects of living in a healthy environment have never before been so dependent on outside forces.

Yet there is much evidence that North Americans have less easy access to good information about the outside world than even a few years ago. Since the end of the Cold War, newspaper and television coverage of events in other countries has dropped dramatically. It is difficult to put much blame on the mass media, however: International news seldom sells any more. There is simply less interest.

It is not surprising, then, that Americans know comparatively little about the outside world. A recent *Los Angeles Times* survey provides a good example: People in eight countries were asked five basic questions about current events of the day. Americans were dead last in their knowledge, trailing people from Canada, Mexico, England, France, Spain, Germany, and Italy.* It is also not surprising that the annual report published by the Swiss World Economic Forum always ranks American executives quite low in their international experience and understanding.

Such ignorance harms American competitiveness in the world economy in many ways. But there is much more. Seymour Martin Lipset put it nicely in one of his recent books: "Those who know only one country know no country" (Lipset 1996: 17). Considerable time spent in a foreign

---

*For example, while only 3 percent of Germans missed all five questions, 37 percent of the Americans did (*Los Angeles Times*, March 16, 1994).

country is one of the best stimulants for a sociological imagination: Studying or doing research in other countries makes us realize how much we really, in fact, have learned about our own society in the process. Seeing other social arrangements, ways of doing things, and foreign perspectives allows for far greater insight into the familiar, our own society. This is also to say that ignorance limits solutions to many of our own serious social problems. How many Americans, for example, are aware that levels of poverty are much lower in all other advanced nations and that the workable government services in those countries keep poverty low? Likewise, how many Americans are aware of alternative means of providing health care and quality education or reducing crime?

We can take heart in the fact that sociology in the United States has become more comparative in recent decades. A comparative approach, of course, was at the heart of classical European sociology during the 1800s. But as sociology was transported from Europe to the United States early in the 20th century, it lost much of this comparative focus. In recent years, sociology journals have published more comparative research. There are large data sets with samples from many countries around the world in research seeking general laws on issues such as the causes of social mobility or political violence, all very much in the tradition of Durkheim. But we also need much more of the old Max Weber. His was a qualitative historical and comparative perspective (Smelser 1976; Ragin and Zaret 1983). Weber's methodology provides a richer understanding of other societies, a greater recognition of the complexity of social, cultural, and historical forces shaping each society. Ahead of his time in many ways, C. Wright Mills was planning a qualitative comparative sociology of world regions just before his death in 1961 (Horowitz 1983:324). [Too few American sociologists have yet to follow in his footsteps.]

Following these trends, sociology textbooks in the United States have also become more comparative in content in recent years. And while this tendency must be applauded, it is not enough. Typically, there is an example from Japan here, another from Germany there, and so on, haphazardly for a few countries in different subject areas as the writer's knowledge of these bits and pieces allows. What we need are the textbook equivalents of a richer Weberian comparative analysis, a qualitative comparative analysis of the social, cultural, and historical forces that have combined to make relatively unique societies around the world. It is this type of comparative material that can best help people in the United States overcome their lack of understanding about other countries and allow them to see their own society with much greater insight.

The Comparative Societies Series, of which this book is a part, has been designed as a small step in filling this need. We have currently selected 12 countries on which to focus: Japan, Thailand, Switzerland, Mexico, Eritria, Hungary, Germany, China, India, Iran, Brazil, and Russia. We selected these countries as representatives of major world regions and cultures, and each will be examined in separate books written by talented sociologists. All of these basic sociological issues and topics will be covered: Each book will begin with a look at the important historical and geographical forces shaping the society, then turn to basic aspects of social organization and culture. From there each book will proceed to examine the political and economic institutions of the specific country, along with the social stratification, the family, religion, education, and finally urbanization, demography, social problems, and social change.

Although each volume in the Comparative Societies Series is of necessity brief to allow for use as supplementary readings in standard sociology courses, we have tried to assure that this brief coverage provides students with sufficient information to better understand each society, as well as their own. The ideal would be to transport every student to another country for a period of observation and learning. Realizing the unfortunate impractically of this ideal, we hope to do the next best thing— to at least mentally move these students to a country very different from their own, provide something of the everyday reality of the people in these other countries, and demonstrate how the tools of sociological analysis can help them see these societies as well as their own with much greater understanding.

Harold R. Kerbo
San Luis Obispo, CA
June 1997

AUTHORS' PREFACE

Germany is a country of seeming contradictions: It is the country of Johann Sebastian Bach, Ludwig van Beethoven, Johann Wolfgang von Goethe, Martin Luther, . . . and Adolf Hitler. Germany has produced some of the greatest social scientists in history (men such as Karl Marx, Max Weber, and Georg Simmel), but also has provided the bedrock of 20th century fascism. Germany has helped set the stage for modern science with the rational philosophies of men such as Immanuel Kant, but also provided leaders for the romantic movement in the arts with the likes of Richard Wagner and Johannes Brahms. In fact, there seems to be movement back and forth between rationalism and romanticism, reason and emotion, throughout German history (Craig 1991).

Few Americans, however, are aware of these contradictions; their knowledge of Germany seems to have a single focus. In most American bookstores, shelves devoted to Germany are dominated by books on World War II, Nazism, Hitler, and the Holocaust. The bookshelves for France, China, Mexico, or any other major country have books on politics, economic issues, religions, and the entire range of subjects that could be expected about a society and nation. It is as if everything else about Germany doesn't matter or never happened. In the American mind, it seems, no other country is so dominated by one subject or such a short period of its history. Young Germans visiting or living in the United States know that no matter whom they meet, the dreaded subject will inevitably come up (Hegi 1997). Nazism and the Holocaust, of course, are among the most tragic events in the history of human societies and certainly among the most excruciating events of the 20th century. However, there is much more to know about Germany and Germans, as there is to know about any country and its people.

Germany today is the major economic power of Europe, representing the world's third largest economy behind the United States and Japan. Germany is also the central member of the European Union, which is growing in size by expanding toward Eastern Europe. Germany prior to 1989 was part of a continent that was largely oriented toward the West and the Atlantic alliance, symbolized by its capital, Bonn, which is located in its western part. The unified Germany will be increasingly oriented toward continental Europe, with its face looking eastward. This is most vividly demonstrated by its new capital, Berlin, located in the eastern part of Germany. It is a country, in short, that Americans need to know better in a world where countries are becoming increasingly intertwined.

Our goal in this little book is to help people outside of Germany develop a deeper understanding of German society and culture. We do so by comparative means, showing not only the similarities and differences between Germany and other modern societies, particularly the United States, but also between the two parts of Germany, united in 1990 after a break of 40 years of societal experimentation—the eastern part under communism and the western part under capitalism.

Chapter 1 introduces some basic information about the geography and population of Germany about basic German values. Chapter 2 summarizes some of the most important aspects of German history, while the remaining chapters have a more direct focus on the present. Chapters 3 and 4 acquaint you with the basic features of the German political system and economy today. Chapter 5 covers the German stratification system, including race and gender inequalities, with an interesting contrast to that of the United States. Then, chapters 6 and 7 explore other German institutions: the family, religion, and education. Chapter 8 presents some of the important social problems facing Germany today, including unemployment, crime, an evolving multicultural population, population growth, and suburbanization. Finally, Chapter 9 describes several important social changes confronting Germany and the emerging European Union on their way into the 21st century, as well as problems brought about by German reunification following the fall of the Berlin Wall in 1989.

We would like to thank several people for their support in putting this book together, especially Claudius Rosenthal, Oliver Sassin, Christina Wasmann, Mark Weinem, Melanie Moennich, and Achim Graf. Our thanks also go to our editors and their assistants at McGraw-Hill who helped make this book and the whole Comparative Societies Series possible through their support and enthusiasm: first Jill Gordon and Amy Smeltzley, and then Sally Constable and Kate Purcell.

As we finish work on this book, it seems fitting for the two authors, one American and the other Austrian (though with 20 years of experience as a university professor in Germany), to reflect back upon the 20th century. Through our discussions over the many years of our friendship we have found that it was quite possible our fathers were not far from each other, on different sides of the battle lines, during World War II. In contrast to all the terrible events of that war, the American author grew up with stories about some ordinary Germans and their kindness toward his father, who was a prisoner of war in Germany during the final months of World War II; and the second author still sees that smiling American soldier presenting the first chocolate bar to the little boy in a small mountain village near Salzburg in 1945. As we look toward the 21st century we can be thankful that the prospects for a peaceful century look much better for our children (Nicole and Emily, Sandra and Mark) than it did for their grandparents. We dedicate this book to all of them.

Harold R. Kerbo
Hermann Strasser
Duisburg, Germany
January 1999

TABLE OF CONTENTS

Editor's Preface   v

Authors' Preface   ix

Chapter 1

An Introduction: Modern Germany in Its Cultural Context   1

Geography and Population   2
Basic German Values   3
   The Nature of Culture and Some Cautions   4
The "Prussian" Core Values   5
Conclusion   8

Chapter 2

The Historical Context   9

The Emergence of European Feudalism   10
Why the West?   11
German Disunity and the Modern World System   12
The First German Unification   14
The State and Economic Development   16
The World System, Colonial Empires, and the Causes of the World Wars   17
The End of World War I and the Rise of National Socialism   18
   Hitler's Supporters   20
German Recovery and the Postwar "Economic Miracle"   22
   The "Economic Miracle"   23
East Germany and the Fall of the Wall   24
Conclusion   26

Chapter 3

The Political System   27

The German Political System   28
   The Democratic Institutions   29
   The Welfare State and Big Government   34
European Unification   39
Conclusion   40

Chapter 4

The Economy   41

German Capitalism   42
Germany's Economic Development after 1945   44
Working in Germany and Worker Influence   46
    Outcomes of German Worker Influence   48
Conclusion   51

Chapter 5

Social Stratification: New Forms of Inequality and Class Relations   52

The Nature of Social Stratification   53
    Reduced Inequality   54
German Workers and Wages   56
A History of German Labor Laws   56
Gender Inequalities   58
Social Mobility and Status Attainment   61
The German Upper Class   63
    Elite Unity   64
Conclusion   66

Chapter 6

The Family   67

The Family System before World War II   68
Postwar Developments   69
Modernity, Affluence, and Their Impact on the Family   70
    New Ways of Living Together   70
The Demography of the German Family   71
    Different Developments in East and West Germany   73
The German Family in a Comparative Context   73
Conclusion   74

Chapter 7

Religion and Education in Germany   76

Religion in Germany   77
    A History of Religion in Germany   78
    The Churches and the State in the Federal Republic Today   81
    The Crisis of the Churches   82

Allah in Germany   83
Sects and the State   85
Conclusion   86
Education in Germany   86
  The Educational System of the Federal Republic   87
  The Educational System of Communist East Germany until 1989   88
  Postwar Educational Expansion: More Opportunities, Less Justice?   89
Conclusion   90

Chapter 8

Social Problems   92

Unemployment and Poverty   93
  Unemployment versus Poverty   96
Crime and Vice   98
  Crime Rate   98
  Sexual Offenses   100
  Drug Abuse   101
Race and Ethnic Discrimination   103
Population Problems   106
Urban Problems: Suburbanization as a Social Problem   108
Conclusion   109

Chapter 9

**Social Change in the New Century: German Transitions
and Post–Cold War Realities   111**

German Unification and Its Consequences   113
  Political Unification   113
  Social and Psychological Unification   114
  Economic Unification   115
European Unification   117
  The European Union's Impact on Germany   119
The Modern World System in Change: The End of the Cold War   120
Conclusion   122

ENDNOTES   124
GLOSSARY   129
REFERENCES   135
INTERNET RESOURCES   149
INDEXES   151

CHAPTER 1

An Introduction

Modern Germany in Its Cultural Context

It is likely that the images of Germany many Americans have continue to be dominated by scenes of World War II. Movies about the war, such as *Saving Private Ryan,* can give a false image of a country that seems to remain old and traditional. The "economic miracle" that brought Germany out of war devastation in the 1960s and 1970s may have altered this image for some Americans, but probably not enough. With the collapse of the Berlin Wall in 1989, however, the new Germany is no doubt being recognized by more and more Americans. And then, in 1998, when German corporations suddenly began buying up big American ones, such as Chrysler, even more Americans have been forced to take notice of the new, modern German nation.

The focus of this book is this new and modern German society, a society that is in many ways the leader of the new European Union, and a society that has the third largest economy in the world. Modern Germany also presents us with a very interesting contrast to the United States. In so many ways German society today is much like that of the United States; but then again, as we will see in this book, it can also be different. Because of the similarities and contrasts between Germany and the United States, comparing the two is very instructive. By considering how German society can be so similar and yet so different from American society, we can learn a great deal more about both societies.

To begin this task, we start with some basic facts about German geography and population. We then move to the important topics of basic German values and social structure, which can help us better understand the many subjects covered in later chapters: the German political system and economy; social stratification; institutions such as religion, the family, and education; and finally social problems and social changes facing Germany past and present.

GEOGRAPHY AND POPULATION

It is again movies that provide most Americans with their visions of German countryside and cities: beautiful mountains and forests, old cathedrals in such cities as Cologne, Bamberg, and Speyer, and spectacular castle ruins along the Rhine, Mosel, Main, and Elbe rivers. In many ways these visions are quite accurate. There are also flat plains and big cities that show modern faces, especially after being rebuilt after the massive bombing of World War II.

As seen on the map opposite page 1, Germany today is located in northwestern Europe. In the north, Germany touches the North Sea and the Baltic Sea, with Denmark at its northern frontier. To the west of Germany we find The Netherlands, Belgium, and Luxemburg. France is to the southwest, and Switzerland and Austria are to the south and southeast. With the inclusion of what until 1989 was East Germany, Germany touches the Czech Republic and Poland to the east. As the map and this description indicate, Germany is a main crossroad between Eastern Europe, the Scandinavian countries, southern Europe, and the countries of what has long been called Western Europe. This location has had a major impact on Germany today and its history.

With 357,000 square kilometers, Germany is smaller in area than France or Spain but has the largest population of Europe (excluding Russia). Germany has approximately 81 million people, substantially more than Italy (58 million) and England (57 million) but considerably less than the United States (265 million) and Japan (140 million). There is an average of 230 people per square kilometer in Germany compared to 116 people per square kilometer for the whole of the European Union. However, in contrast to many other modern industrial societies, Germany is more of a small town country. The largest metropolitan area, Berlin, has only about 3.5 million people, compared to large metropolitan areas of other countries such as New York, Los Angeles, Cairo, and Tokyo, all with more than 10 million people.

Finally, it is useful to note that in contrast to the United States, there is less ethnic diversity in Germany. This, as we will see later, has recently been changing with hundreds of thousands of immigrants coming into Germany. Now Germany has more foreigners within its borders than other nations in Europe. At the end of the 1990s, there were 8.5 million people in Germany, or 11 percent of the population, who were **ethnic minorities** (regardless of whether they had German citizenship or not). Turks represent the largest group with more than 2 million, or 2.5 percent of the population (Schmalz-Jacobsen and Hansen 1997: 164). By comparison, 9 percent of the U.S. population was born in a foreign country, while about 25 percent can be considered ethnic minorities.

BASIC GERMAN VALUES

When traveling through Europe, Americans are sometimes amazed by another kind of diversity: There are significant differences from country to country in Europe despite the small scale of the geopolitical setting. Imagine driving from, say, New York to New Hampshire or from Oklahoma to Georgia and finding totally different languages, driving habits, and differences in important values. Such is the case when traveling, for example, from Germany to Holland or from Germany to northern France. One can sense different attitudes: The Dutch, for example, may seem somewhat more friendly, easy going, and informal in social interactions than do Germans. Many national laws also reflect different preferences between the two countries, such as no speed limits on the Autobahn in Germany. Germans, in contrast to most other Europeans, are seen (and see themselves) as being very organized and in many ways overregulated. Opinion polls of foreign tourists indicate much agreement that German people are more difficult to get to know and among the least friendly in Europe, while the Italians and Spanish are rated the most friendly (*Los Angeles Times*, May 20, 1996).

Such differences are also recognized by Europeans: Throughout history they have assigned character types and generalizations to each other. A longstanding joke, with perhaps some useful generalizations,

Like the rest of Europe, and in contrast to the United States, Germany is a society with a mixture of the old and the new. For example, this photo shows part of the new art museum in Köln (Cologne) with the famous old Gothic Cathedral in the background, which dates back to the 13th century but was actually completed only in 1843–80.

says: Heaven is where the police are British, the chefs are French, the mechanics German, the lovers Italian, and it's all organized by the Swiss. Hell is where the police are German, the chefs British, the mechanics French, the lovers Swiss, and it's all organized by the Italians. Or as an 18th century writer put it even back then, "Every nation has its principal motive. In Germany it is obedience; in England, freedom; in Holland, trade; in France, the honor of the king." One can agree with the German reputation for mechanical skills, though disagree in recent decades with the put-down to German police. While certainly overgeneralized, such European attitudes do suggest certain differences in national character that must be given some recognition.

The Nature of Culture and Some Cautions

Many differences between countries in Europe are related to what is usually, and loosely, called **culture.** Other differences are often related to aspects of **social structure:** how people and groups are tied together in society. In this section we focus on **value orientations,** which are crucial to understanding culture, the total way of life of a people.

Before proceeding, however, we must sound three notes of caution about cultural explanations of behavior. First, cultural values are rather vague: In practice they need interpretation in terms of rules and situations to see how they apply. Second, cultural values are subject to change, especially over time. This has been the case in Germany between the 1960s and the 1980s when "materialistic values" (for example, economic prosperity, belief in authority, maintaining order) were replaced, at least partially, by "postmaterialistic values" (such as self-realization, freedom, quality of life). This hypothesis, as presented time and again by Ronald Inglehart (1989; 1996), essentially asserts that in an individualizing society such as Germany the politics (and rhetoric) of distribution are supplanted by a politics of values. For example, in the course of modernization, religious and communal values shifted in the direction of achievement motivation and the preference for rational-legal rules. In the postmodern era there is a tendency to replace mere achievement with the holistic idea of self-realization.

Third, not all people within a particular society equally accept the values of the dominant culture. With respect to Germany, the best example has been the social experiment of the two German states, which went on for 40 years. While some basic German cultural orientations remain, the East Germans, who grew up under a communist dictatorship, have some value orientations not shared by their West German cousins. Thus, Germans in East and West tend to focus on different values—social versus liberal values (solidarity and authority versus individualism and self-responsibility)—except in cases where situational experiences have led to different attitudes as exemplified by East Germans who are hit by unemployment and hence are less content (Bellers and Bellers 1997; Zelle

1998). Even with all of these cautions, we do find cultural values are useful in helping us understand people from different societies.

THE "PRUSSIAN" CORE VALUES

As the well-known American scholar of German history Gordon Craig points out, there has been extensive change in the German "national character" since 1945, but some basic values and traditions remain (Craig 1991:11). Compared to people from other western nations of Europe and North America, Germans are often described as strongly favoring order and predictability, respect for authority, diligence, and status ranking.

One indicator of the above is the multitude of official rules governing all kinds of behavior in Germany. There are rules pertaining to the size of trash cans, hours of the day when bottles can be dropped in the recycling bin, and when showers can be taken and laundry done in apartments. There is the Emission Protection Law (Immissionsschutzgesetz), which mandates such things as quiet times (no noise above 25 decibels)—between 1 PM and 3 PM when people might be taking naps, as well as between 10 PM and 6 AM; and there is the Neighbor Rights Law (Nachbarrechtsgesetz), which governs such things as the size of hedges and when lawns can be mown (the time and day), as well as other things about a person's property.

Along with the inclination toward social order comes the traditional German preference toward status ranking and the status order. While by no means as conscious of status ranking as the Japanese, Germans have a formality, respect for authority, and fondness for titles not found, for instance, in the United States. A university professor, for example, is still often referred to as Herr Professor while his wife can be called Frau Professor (or simply the wife of Professor so and so). There is also a continued use of old aristocratic titles such as Fuerst (prince) and Baron to a greater extent in Germany than elsewhere in Europe (Ardagh 1987:153).

The common assumption is that this love for rules and social order is deeply rooted in Prussian culture, which, as we will see in our next chapter, goes back many centuries. It is also commonly assumed that this love for order is in large part responsible for many other things in Germany, from a tendency toward **ethnocentrism** and **racism** to the "postwar economic miracle."

While there is little doubt about the German tendency toward order, one can, however, question its sources and outcomes. Some historians argue that it results from a natural reserve and an uneasiness about the past. Others believe that it originated more recently and stems primarily from breaks in the social order in Germany's recent past: for example, the Thirty Years War of 1618 to 1648 when 35 percent of the population was killed; the economic collapses of the 1920s and in the wake of the Great Depression of the 1930s, which set the stage for Hitler and

Burying Hoppeditz: Like European nations with a large Catholic population, Germans celebrate during the Carnival season, much like Mardi Gras is celebrated in New Orleans. As a central figure of customs in the Rhineland part of Germany, Hoppeditz symbolizes carnival license. He is awaken each year on November 11, 11:11 a.m., gives a speech in which he presents people a mirror by scorning all weaknesses and sins that he observed during the past year without denouncing individuals. On Ash Wednesday, as the photo shows, he "dies" while the fools bemourn him and put him symbolically to rest or burn him.

the rise of National Socialism; not to mention the two world wars in this century (Craig 1991; Bendix 1978; Raff 1988). Whatever the cause, and whenever this cluster of Prussian values developed, there is evidence for the existence of these value orientations in Germany today.

One of the most interesting studies suggesting differing value orientations around the world was conducted by Geert Hofstede (1991). With responses from over 15,000 people in 53 countries, he ranked these countries on several basic value orientations. For example, one of the most general value orientations is commonly described as an **individualistic value system** versus a **collectivistic value system.** This simply means that the group and society are more important in a collectivist system, and the individual must submit to the needs and rules of the group to a greater extent than people living in a country with an individualist value system. Hofstede (1991:53) found people in the United States to be the most individualistic of all, scoring an average 91 on his individualism index (with 100 being the perfect score). People from Australia, England, Canada, The Netherlands, and New Zealand were ranked just below the United States on this index, while people in Asian countries such as Thailand, Singapore, Hong Kong, South Korea, Taiwan, and Malaysia scored much lower. Germans, however, scored toward the middle of this index, suggesting a greater group orientation than most other western countries (also see Hampden-Turner and Trompenaars 1993:16).

The uncertainty avoidance scale used by Hofstede is also quite interesting. This scale measures the extent to which people can live with or accept uncertainty in contrast to strongly avoiding uncertainty. Americans and the British are very low on this scale (accepting uncertainty), while Germans are high for western nations (least accepting of uncertainty). The stress on order and rules in Germany is no doubt a reflection of this value orientation (Hofstede 1991:126). It may even be that the great German sociologist Max Weber, who wrote extensively about the logic of bureaucracies, was biased by this German value orientation. It seems that Max Weber (1947) overestimated the need for rather rigid and impersonal rules within bureaucracies and, thus, underestimated today's trend toward more flexibility in corporate organizations.

Finally, Hofstede's measure of a long-term versus short-term value orientation is worth noting. People with a long-term value orientation are more concerned with planning and what will happen, say, 10 years from now than are people with a short-term value orientation, who are more likely to focus on the present. Most Asian nations score high on the long-term orientation, while the United States and England score among the lowest. Again, Germany is in the middle, generally between clusters of Asian nations and western nations.

We conclude this section by suggesting why it is important to be aware of the differing value orientations described above. First of all, value orientations have important consequences for how German society works; in Chapter 5, for example, its mobility and labor market regimes operate quite differently than those in the United States. Second, as countries become more interlinked, especially economically, people from different countries must work together to a much greater extent than ever before. Understanding the value orientations of others makes for much less conflict and more successful joint endeavors.

In research conducted in Germany, for example, we found that several Japanese corporations were having extensive conflicts between Japanese managers and German employees because some basic value differences were not well understood or respected by either side (Kerbo, Wittenhagen, and Nakao 1994a, 1994b). Another useful lesson comes with the current unification of Europe, which we examine later in this book. The unification is not proceeding smoothly, to a large degree, because of different priorities in solving problems based on differing value orientations of European nations.

The Germans, for example, tend to stress order and the creation of more rules in everything from worker welfare, financial restructuring, and product standards to environmental protection, while the more individualistic British and less orderly Italians oppose some of these rules. During the latter 1990s, with a new common currency (the Euro) and central European banking system coming into existence, the Germans' preference for avoiding uncertainty has led them to demand that economic standards, including public debt, be adopted to ensure a stable currency. These rules are opposed by people and governments of many other member states of the European Union because these rules can mean less government spending and higher unemployment. One result has been massive demonstrations in France and elsewhere in recent years, with many more likely.

CONCLUSION

With the fall of communism in Russia and Eastern Europe in the early 1990s, Germany is in a geographical position to build bridges to these nations that it was separated from by the Cold War for almost 50 years. Because Germany has the strongest economy in Europe, and the third largest in the world behind the United States and Japan, Germany will be one of the most important nations shaping the future of the world economy and the place of European nations within it. However, the future of European unification and the world economy also depends upon a better understanding of the differences in culture and social structure among the world's leading nations.

In this introductory chapter we described some characteristics of modern Germany and its people. To make all of this more understandable, however, we have more to cover. We need insight into the German history that has shaped the current German culture and social structure, and we need to understand what Germany means to her European neighbors. To help with this task, the next chapter provides a short review of relevant aspects of recent German history.

CHAPTER 2

The Historical Context

In an opinion poll taken soon after World War II, Americans were asked whom they thought the United States could work more closely with after the war, Japan or Germany. By an overwhelming majority Americans said Germany. And the responses remained for years in follow-up polls, even after details of the **Holocaust** became well known. The results of the survey were most likely affected by the fact that more Americans have immigrated from Germany than anywhere else except England: A large percentage of the American population, in other words, has relatives who made them feel at least somewhat attached to the old country.

For the most part, however, these relatives are fairly old or dead: While between 18 and 40 percent of Americans say they have some German ethnic heritage (depending on the region of the United States), the vast majority of German immigrants came to the United States before the 20th century. By 1900 the percentage of immigrants coming from northern and western Europe had dropped below 50 percent, and in 20 more years the percentage was below 17 percent and falling fast (Hraba 1994). The point is, of course, that by 1945 few Americans directly knew much about Germany, its history, and traditions. With the exception of events around World War II, unfortunately, the situation has changed little since then.

The present chapter is designed to provide some basic background information about the history of German society that will make information in the following chapters much easier to comprehend. In a small book such as this, of course, we will not cover all or even much of German history. Sociologists, however, must understand important aspects of the past in order to know where the society under study stands at present, how it has developed thus far, and which course it will likely take in the future.

Several questions guide our review of German history: Who are the Germans and where do their traditions come from? Why was Germany so late in developing and modernizing compared to most other countries in Western Europe, and why was Germany able to develop so fast once it had taken off? What provoked World Wars I and II, and, of course, what accounts for the rise of Hitler's National Socialism? And, finally, what caused German society to change so dramatically after World War II, and in what ways has it changed?

THE EMERGENCE OF EUROPEAN FEUDALISM

Historical and archeological information suggests that the first people resided in what is now Germany about 4,000 years ago, at the beginning of the Bronze Age. They were of Indo-Germanic origin. Since that time, waves of various invaders flooded between the Alps and the North Sea and Baltic Sea with the last most permanent occupiers being the Romans during the reign of the Roman Empire, from about 50 BC to 400 AD (Davies 1996; Raff 1988).

It is with the fall of the Roman Empire, however, that we should begin with a bit more detail about early German history, as well as that of Europe more generally. Lasting from about 500 BC until 500 AD, the Roman Empire did at least bring stability and social order to Europe. However, it collapsed in the face of much inequality and exploitation (with a push by various invaders) by 500 AD, and what we now think of as Europe entered a time of instability and lack of change known as the Dark Ages (Davies 1996; Wells 1971; Brunt 1971; Jones 1974). This *was* a time of regress and backwardness compared to many other places in the world, particularly Arab and Asian civilizations. For example, there were hardly any advancements in art, science, or technology in Europe during this time, and indeed very few people at all could read or write. The center of political, economic, and cultural attention turned to the east, to the Byzantium civilization (Clark 1969).

Slowly, however, in a few hundred years, some order and advancement emerged in Europe, made possible by a new form of social organization called **feudalism.** Feudalism is an agrarian system with most land held by wealthy owners and most other people attached to the land of the feudal lord as serfs or peasants. This agrarian system of economic and political organization emerged in Europe as people came together seeking protection and cooperation after the fall of the Roman Empire.

At first, very small enclaves of people came into existence, living on the manor, or the land of the first small feudal lords. Over the centuries, however, in a process of conquest and consolidation, some feudal manors came to rule over others, eventually forming what can be described as small kingdoms. Some two hundred years after the Romans had moved out of Northern and Central Europe, around 250 AD, the Kingdom of the Franks had already started to form (Davies 1996; Raff 1988). By 800 AD, the Kingdom of the Franks covered most of Europe and was led by the first truly famous king, Charlemagne. Soon, however, the first big division came when the "Holy Roman Empire of the German

Nation" split from the Kingdom of the Franks in 962 AD. Soon afterward, about 1000 AD, other nations such as France, Italy, and England began to take shape.

Germany, as we recognize it today, however, was hindered in this nation-forming process. It was not until the late 1800s that a consolidated Germany finally appeared. Why this consolidation took so long and the effects it had upon Germany today are subjects of considerable importance. But we need to make a diversion from Germany more specifically, to Western Europe more broadly, to consider the question of why and how modernization and industrialization happened first in this part of the world.

WHY THE WEST?

One of the central questions for social scientists has always been why what we call modernization and industrialization developed first in the West and, more specifically, in northwestern Europe beginning roughly about 1500 AD. (This is the time when Italian Christopher Columbus, employed by the Spanish, discovered America, others sailed to the Far Eastern shores, and the Arabs were ousted from the Iberian peninsula.) This question is of critical importance to sociologists because its answer helps us understand some of the basic differences in the political economies of this part of the world, which set the stage for the takeoff of modernization. The question becomes even more intriguing when we note that China at around this time was ahead of the West in many types of science and technology. China, however, was to stagnate and decline until Mao and the Communist Revolution in the mid-20th century began to destroy the impediments to change in China.

Among some of the most fundamental differences in northwestern Europe around 1500 compared to China involve climate and geography (Chirot 1984, 1986). For one thing, Europe is divided by many rivers and mountains, natural boundaries that promoted separate nations. In contrast, the vast central plains of what is now China literally paved the way for a huge imperial government. The numerous small nations in Europe encouraged trial and competition, while China's central government dominated wide regions and imposed a rather uniform system of rules and traditions. Out of this central government in China came protection for dominant elites who preferred things to stay as they were because their power and privilege depended upon keeping the status quo.

Equally important, different forms of agriculture developed in northwestern Europe and China. The wet rice agriculture of China required large construction projects and water systems for the large quantities of water needed, which again meant to require a strong central state (Kennedy 1987:xvi), creating what some call "hydraulic empires" (Wittfogel 1957). Northwestern Europe, in contrast, survived mostly on cereal grains, such as wheat, which could be cultivated without involving groups and overarching government or community infrastructure projects. As a consequence, early European governments never became as dominant as those in China and, though they often tried, were ultimately unable to prevent social change as effectively as did the Chinese imperial government.

Finally, with respect to climate and geography we should note that a favorable European climate helped maintain a balance of humans and animals to the amount of land, unlike many other places in the world (Chirot 1984). Some scholars even suggest that the black death played an important part in all of this. The climate and conditions of the time allowed for the spread of the black death in Europe from 1000 to 1500 AD, in some areas killing over half the population but resulting in a land-to-population ratio more favorable to economic development.

Many early sociologists, such as Max Weber (1858–1920), however, argued that religious values and ideas were more important reasons why northwestern Europe became the first industrial and modernized part of the world. While we may disagree whether these factors were as important as Weber claimed, they did have some influence. As our discussion of the Protestant Reformation in the following section shows, these ideas are useful in understanding the early history of Germany.

According to Weber (1958) in his famous book, *The Protestant Ethic and the Spirit of Capitalism,* it was the Protestant religion that provided a new world view, a new way of thinking about the place of the individual and the meaning of life, and that motivated a turn toward capitalism and subsequently spurred industrialization. In short, compared to Catholicism, Protestantism is a more individualistic religion, allowing for more independence and innovation. It was fueled by Calvinism's new view of salvation. According to this view, humans, in essence, were predestined at birth to be among the saved or condemned to hell. However, the only way to figure out which side one would be on was by success in this life. Given that success was being defined in economic terms, people reasoned that those who become rich must be among the saved. Along with material success, Calvinism handed down a philosophy of asceticism— that is, a belief that wealth was not to be spent on "wine, women, and song," but to be saved and reinvested in new production capacities. Hence, Weber argued that the spirit of capitalism was grounded, for some time at least, in the Protestant ethic. This Protestant ethic spread throughout northwestern Europe to Sweden, England, Holland, and, of course, northern Germany. While these other countries were at the forefront of modernization and industrialization by the 1600s and 1700s, Germany faced other barriers.

GERMAN DISUNITY AND THE MODERN WORLD SYSTEM

What is called the **modern world system** began to take shape about 1500 AD (Chirot 1986; Wallerstein 1974, 1980, 1989). In contrast to the previous world empires such as the Roman or Chinese empires, which were based upon military power and glory-seeking emperors, the new modern world system was based more upon economic competition and rational calculation. The beginning of the modern world system and the exploration for riches was stimulated by poor economic conditions in Europe during the 1400s, and also by the Protestant Reformation, important technological inventions, and rumors about distant paradises (Kennedy 1987; Raff 1988). As the ships from Spain and Portugal, and later from England, Holland, and France, set out to conquer and exploit new worlds and their people, the riches brought back contributed to an expanding European economy and to overcoming the economic slump of the 1400s. However, while Spain and Portugal started the process of colonizing third world people, they were unable to do so with as much efficiency and economic gain in the long run as the countries of northwestern Europe, who became the dominant economic and military powers of the world until World War I.

To the extent that Weber was correct about the Protestant ethic stimulating capitalism and economic growth, it is ironic to note that at first Germany profited much less from the development of the modern world system and the economic expansion it helped bring about in Europe. It was Martin Luther, a German priest, who started the Protestant Reformation in the early 1500s against the dominance of the Catholic Church. But unlike Holland and England where the Protestant Reformation resulted in an extensive rejection of the Catholicism of the elites, a countermovement emerged in Germany to assure the continued dominance of Catholicism, especially in the southern regions of Germany.

For our subject, however, what is most important is that the Protestant Reformation and the ensuing Counter-Reformation created even stronger divisions in Germany. These divisions also set the stage for the Thirty Years War (1618–1648), which resulted in the deaths of more than a third of the German population, and more hate and conflict between the people of different regions of Germany (Craig 1991:20). Unlike France, England, and Holland, Germany could not generate the unity needed to get back on its feet economically and to promote further economic development. At one point as many as 300 separate Germanic territories existed. By the late 1700s, Frederick the Great was able to create a stronger and more unified Prussia in northern and eastern Germany, but this was still not sufficient for the needed economic expansion.

The 1700s were also the time when Germany, like much of Europe, experienced the "Enlightenment Age," led by some of the greatest German intellectuals such as Goethe, Schiller, and Kant. But unlike many other European nations, especially France, in Germany no political revolution followed the Enlightenment. The old political blocks to economic development remained. The old aristocracy in connection with the monarch and the army effectively prevented policies that would stimulate economic expansion and ultimately move the new capitalist class of merchants to economic dominance and eventually to political power

(Bendix 1978; Kerbo 1996:72–74). In France, for example, the French Revolution of 1789 destroyed the old political system dominated by the feudal aristocrats. Along with the American Revolution, this was the signal for political upheavals all over Europe.

Such an uprising never happened in Germany, or at least not for a long time. Rather, what occurred in Germany were some mild reforms under what was called the Reform Edict of 1807. As a result of the reforms, peasants were freed from serfdom (meaning they could move from their current landlord and seek other jobs); the freedom to enter other occupations was established; in 1808, self-governing bodies were introduced; in 1810, the freedom of trade act was enacted; in 1809–10, the renowned reform of the educational system took effect; and, finally, due to Napoleon's occupation, the army was reorganized between 1807 and 1814. To make things even more difficult for Germany, after France and Napoleon were finally defeated by the other European powers, the Viennese Congress of 1815 further divided Germany to ensure greater English power.

The old aristocracy in Germany is best represented by the **Junker** class, ridiculed as "German mandarins" by writers such as Jacob Grimm. In essence the Junker class was a landed aristocracy with only regional functions and traditional privileges of descent in the army, the diplomatic service, and public administration. This situation prompted the French politician Honoré de Mirabeau to comment: "Other states have an army. Prussia is an army which owns a state." Germany was unique among the European powers of the day in the extent to which this class remained powerful throughout the 1800s, and even into the early 20th century (Wehler 1995:169–172; Moore 1966; Raff 1988:189). In short, the Junker class helped keep Germany divided both into little kingdoms and social niches where they held power. This prevented the development of a modern state that could unify Germany and create a more competitive economy and bring Germany into a position of power in the modern world system. In many respects, Germany thus emerges as a "belated nation." While industrialization took off in Great Britain around 1785, in France in the 1830s, and in the United States in 1845, Germany, it is said, did not feel the initial effects of modernity before the middle of the 19th century (cf. Kiesewetter 1996; McMulhall 1969). As mentioned already, the reasons for the delay are too numerous to list. Among them certainly is the mercantilistic economy that focused on the limited interests of small territories and the feudal order of society, which only slowly began to change with the reforms of Freiherr vom Stein and Fürst Hardenberg.

THE FIRST GERMAN UNIFICATION

The first German unification, which occurred in the second half of the 1800s, was one of the most important events in German as well as European history. This unification not only helped create rapid economic de-

Germany is noted for its many beautiful castles dating back several centuries, such as the Burg Eltz located on the Mosel river shown here. Until the late 19th century Germany, remained a country divided into many small feudal "kingdoms," more than any other European nation and each little "kingdom" with castles for the nobility ruling over their sections of the German territories.

velopment in Germany, but also set the stage for World Wars I and II in the 20th century. Given the importance of this first unification, it is certainly worth describing, at least in brief.

The push for unifying the various Germanic territories began in the early 1800s, mostly by social movements made up of intellectuals and students, that is, people less tied to the old social structures. These were also the people who could more clearly see how disunity was harming Germany's economic competitiveness with other European powers. These movements did stimulate the German Customs Union by 1834, a union that brought about some free movement of commerce around the German territories but had no political union behind it. The union's *spiritus rector*, the economist Friedrich List, who was forced to emigrate to the United States in 1825 and returned several years later, had something else in mind when he talked about the "Siamese twin": the German Customs Union and expansion of the railway net. While the former guaranteed free trade, the second provided work and income for thousands and began to link coal mines and steel factories, producers and consumers, country and town, low lands and high lands, and provinces and capitals. The railway net exposed the numerous political borders as *the* obstacles to economic development and individual freedom.

Then came the revolts of 1848 all over Europe. In France and elsewhere, these revolts were fueled mostly by an emerging working class

angry over worsening economic conditions. There were attempts by socialist groups to take over parts of France; their foremost theorist, Karl
Marx (1818–1883), was involved after he had been expelled from his native Germany (McLellan 1973). In Germany, by contrast, the social movements gained more support from the rising **bourgeoisie** (middle class
merchants and small capitalists), students, and intellectuals (including
the likes of the great opera composer Richard Wagner). The goal of these
movements was German unification rather than reforms favoring the
working class. But again, the call for German unification met with no
success.

Some 20 years later, however, conditions were finally ripe for unity,
and two men were in the right place to bring it to fruition. The first did
so only indirectly, while the second was an integral part. The first was
Giuseppe Garibaldi, who led Italy to unification. This gave hope to those
calling for unification in Germany. The second was the famous Otto von
Bismarck (1815–98), who brought Germany to unification in 1871 after
succeeding in the "German Unification Wars" of 1864, 1866, and 1870–71.

Bismarck was named prime minister of Prussia under King William I
of Prussia in 1862. In contrast to a somewhat liberal image gained later
because of his establishment of one of the most complete welfare systems
in Europe, Bismarck was a conservative who supported the monarch and
the military elite. However, his most important goal was the political and
not just the economic unity of Germany. King William I was convinced
of the need for unity by Bismarck. However, Prussia was blocked by
Austria, the other large Germanic power, which resisted unity under
Prussian dominance. Bismarck guided Prussia toward war with Austria,
and the Prusso-Austrian War of 1866, which Bismarck won for Prussia,
cleared the way. Shortly thereafter, the Franco-Prussian War of 1870–71
led to the defeat of France and regained old territory for Germany. This
war was the climax of German unity in 1871.

THE STATE AND ECONOMIC DEVELOPMENT

Before leaving this epoch of German history, we should acknowledge
Bismarck's contribution to the modernization of Germany and subsequently to the development of the welfare state. The health and accident
insurance programs he created in the 1880s, and then the disability and
old age insurance programs he created by 1889, became models for the
world. Even the United States, under Franklin Roosevelt in the 1930s,
copied much from Bismarck's welfare programs. But as noted above,
these programs were of less concern to Bismarck than the political unity
of Germany. The welfare programs were more of an afterthought to appease poor workers who were protesting at the time and to neutralize
the labor movement and the social democrats who were opposing Bismarck in the Reichstag. As Piven and Cloward (1971) have pointed out,
welfare benefits for the poor and working class come primarily because

of protest and are given by the ruling elites in an attempt to appease the poor and stop protest.

More than anything else, however, it was rapid economic development that Bismarck brought about with state modernization. However, according to most classical economic theory (and the theory still popular in the United States today), the state has "no business getting involved in business"(Fallows 1994; Thurow 1991; Dietrich 1991). But much like Japan at about the same time (Johnson 1982; Kerbo and McKinstry 1995, 1998), through government planning, economic incentives to business, and state-directed loans, the newly unified government bureaucracy pushed Germany into economic competition with the rest of Europe.

A few figures and an anecdote illustrate the point: In 1890 when Bismarck left office and the German **capitalist development state** was just getting into action, Germany produced 89 million tons of coal. By 1914 Germany was second only to England with 277 million tons of coal production a year (Kennedy 1987:210). In steel production, during this period Germany moved ahead of all countries and produced more steel than England, France, and Russia combined. And in newly emerging technologies such as electronics, optics, and chemicals, the now giant German firms such as Siemens, Bayer, and AEG took the lead. By this time, Germany was only behind England and the United States in overall production, and accounted for 17 percent of the world's manufacturing output (Chirot 1977:25). It is no wonder that British politicians and business leaders at the time were worried about the future economic position of the United Kingdom. Already in the 1880s they passed a law specifying that goods coming from German shores had to carry the label "Made in Germany." The law was accompanied by a campaign against the allegedly low quality of German products.

THE WORLD SYSTEM, COLONIAL EMPIRES, AND THE CAUSES OF THE WORLD WARS

An astute student looking at economic figures, a world map, and understanding the new economic constellation of the late 1800s could easily have predicted disaster. Much of the economic strength of the leading European powers of the time came from colonial exploitation. England, of course, had the biggest colonial empire around the world, while other countries such as France, Belgium, and Holland had colonial systems of a more focused kind in Africa and Asia. But there were other newly emerging economic powers—most importantly, Germany, Italy, and Japan— who started their modernization and economic development late in the 1800s and had few if any colonies. The United States was also one of these newly developing nations, but it needed no colonies because of the vast territories to its west that it could take from the American Indians.

Germany, Italy, and Japan, in contrast, wanted access to raw materials around the world as the British and others before them had taken from native peoples through colonization. The problem, however, could be clearly seen by our student with the map: The current colonial powers already held almost 85 percent of the world, and little worth taking remained (Chirot 1986; Kennedy 1987). This meant that if valuable property was to be conquered, it would most likely have to come from a European power who had stolen it years earlier from native people. It was the German attempt in the early 1900s to acquire more territory and allies that stimulated World War I, and then the German, Italian, and Japanese attempts to do so again in the 1930s that stimulated World War II.

With our focus on Germany, we should explain more fully why Germany had no colonies. The first reason goes back as far as the 1648 Treaty of Westphalia with other European powers that ended the Thirty Years War and legalized splitting up the German territories into hundreds of single states. This left German states landlocked (Raff 1988:193). Then, as explained above, divisions in Germany and its late economic development prevented it from establishing colonial ties earlier. Germany got a few "pieces" of Africa in the 1880s, some little Pacific islands, and a little dot in China in 1889, but that was it (Chirot 1986:76–80). This was almost nothing compared to the colonies held by the other European powers.

After the first German unification in 1871, the German elite wanted its share of colonies. Hence, Germany began to expand its fleet, awakening a nationalist mass movement. Bismarck, seeing the likely outcome and oriented toward compromise with the European powers, resisted. This and other matters put Bismarck in a dispute with the King, and Bismarck resigned his position in 1890. There was worry throughout Europe over his resignation because of the possible new direction that Germany's foreign policy would take, a direction leading to conflict. And as it turned out, they were correct (Raff 1988).

THE END OF WORLD WAR I AND THE RISE OF NATIONAL SOCIALISM

We turn now to one of the most tragic periods of the 20th century, the rise of Hitler and the Nazi Party (officially the **National Socialist Party of Germany**). Our intent, however, is not to join the popular academic game of trying to show how much the German people knew about what the Nazis were doing, or what flaws there might be in the German national character, as represented most recently in Daniel Goldhagen's book, *Hitler's Willing Executioners* (1996). Rather, the sociological questions we consider are related to the conditions that allowed for the rise of a **fascist** government in Germany. Three questions are most important: Why was Germany predisposed to fascism at the time? What had stimulated the move to fascism? And how was the Nazi Party able to take advantage of the situation to gain popular support and to attain political power?

The answer to the first question, why was Germany predisposed to fascism, is somewhat complex, but we will be brief. In one of the most respected sociological works on the subject, Barrington Moore (1966) was able to show that the underlying class structure of a society influences the movement toward either democracy or dictatorship. With a thorough analysis of countries such as Japan, Germany, France, and Russia, Moore reasoned that when their economic development began, both Japan and Germany were alike in having a rather weak middle class or capitalist class, a poorly organized working class, and power still in the hands of the old elites. We have seen that Germany's economic development was pushed by a government strongly influenced not only by a king, but also by the **Junker** aristocracy. In Japan, there was also a kind of top-down revolution in 1868, called the *Meiji Restoration,* which involved old samurai elites taking control of the country and directing state-dominated economic development.

A key point in Moore's analysis is that during Germany's economic crisis there was neither a middle class (capitalist class) nor a working class strong enough to keep the country on the road to democracy. Rather, a fascist group, usually recruited from parts of the old and new *Mittelstand* (small shop owners and white collar workers), as well as the old and new elites, took power, stopped democracy, and made changes favoring the interests of these classes (Strasser 1993). The similarities to Japan (except for the hysterical racism of German Nazis) are striking. Both countries enjoyed a brief period of democracy (called the *Taisho Democracy* in Japan and the Weimar Republic in Germany) which could not last for long.

Germany's brief period of democracy after World War I, the **Weimar Republic,** was named after the first meeting place of the German National Assembly, which gave the new state its constitution after the defeat of World War I and the abduction of the monarch. The Weimar Republic was primarily destroyed by economic crises and the skirmish of political parties, but also by the psychological consequences of the penalties forced upon Germany by the victors of World War I in the Treaty of Versailles. The sociological master, Max Weber, was a member of the German delegation to the peace conference, but left in distress predicting that the concessions placed upon Germany would ruin the economy and cause further crises (Marianne Weber 1975). Weber, as it turned out, was all too perceptive.

The Treaty of Versailles forced Germany to pay substantial war reparations to allied countries and to hand over some of the richest areas of the country to France.[1] The economy soon collapsed with a devastating depreciation of the currency in 1923. Making things worse, the German government began printing more money in a futile attempt to stave off further collapse, creating unbelievable inflation (Raff 1988:243). During 1919, for example, the German mark was 8.9 to the U.S. dollar; by early 1923 the mark was 17,972 to the dollar, and in late 1923 it was 4.2 billion (!)

to the dollar. Some economic reforms brought a mild recovery and reduced inflation for the short "Golden Twenties" in the middle of the decade, as depicted by novelist F. Scott Fitzgerald in *The Great Gatsby* (1924). The Great Depression beginning in 1929 hurt Germany even more than the United States. This long period of economic and political crises, and the humiliation to German national pride, set the stage for Hitler and National Socialism (the Nazi Party) by the early 1930s.

After World War I in 1923, Hitler first tried to take power with a failed *coup d'état* (*Hitler-Putsch*). He was arrested and sent to jail where he wrote his racist manifesto *Mein Kampf* (My Fight), which presented National Socialism as a political religion (Bärsch 1998). With the worsening economic situation, increasing political tensions, and social disintegration, Hitler along with other members of the Nazi Party were eventually elected to the parliament, the **Reichstag,** in 1931. Again, in 1932, the National Socialists won elections, this time attaining 37 percent of the national vote, thus becoming the largest party in the parliament. As the leader of the party with the most seats in the Reichstag, Hitler was appointed chancellor in early 1933 by President Hindenburg, a monarchist and highly decorated veteran of World War I. Representatives of the big industrialists and the landowning aristocrats had agreed to a "solution Hitler." Hitler used his position for political maneuvering to gain more power for himself and to create a totalitarian one-party state.

Almost immediately from the time Hitler took power, the Nazis began their attacks upon Jews as scapegoats for Germany's crisis. They also made plans to claim and eventually take territory from other countries in Europe. The exact steps leading to World War II in Europe we leave to history books. We close this discussion of the pre–World War II period of German history, however, with a sociological attempt to explain why so many Germans, and which ones, supported Hitler.

Hitler's Supporters

It is often assumed that extremist movements, particularly those of the right, are most supported by the lower classes and less educated. In Germany, as in most countries (including the United States militia movements of the 1990s and throughout history), this is not necessarily the case (Lipset and Raab 1970). Research by leading sociologists who fled from Germany to the United States, such as Hans Gerth (1969), also indicates the contrary. While Hitler's supporters came from all walks of life, the working class in Germany was actually underrepresented among active supporters and voters for the Nazi Party. White collar employees and even professional people, along with the young, were much more likely to be active Nazi supporters. The German working class was, relatively speaking, more supportive of the Social Democrats and the Catholic *Zentrum* party (Oberschall 1973:110–11).

As might be expected, there was a tendency for those who fell economically and politically over the years to be clearly more in favor of the Nazis—in other words, those most hurt by Germany's military defeat and economic decline and those most fearful for their livelihoods and most hopeful for their careers. But in the massive depression during the late 1920s and early 1930s in Germany, members of any class were vulnerable to that situation. Even intellectuals and artists and especially public school teachers were supportive of the Nazis (Hamilton 1971; Gerth 1969). If any characterization can be made, in addition to those harmed by economic crisis, it was people from small towns and rural areas, on the one hand, and large parts of the old elite and of the lower middle class, on the other, who were most supportive of the Nazis, especially in the early years (Oberschall 1973:110–11). In other words, the old elite saw in Hitler's National Socialism a means to regain lost social status, as in the case of the Junkers and the officers' corps, or to be elevated to leadership positions. In addition, the delayed industrialization of Germany threatened the achieved status of large parts of the lower middle class of small shopkeepers, artisans, and lower echelon white collar workers (Strasser 1993).

An even more interesting question is whether or not the rich and powerful of Germany, especially industrial magnates, supported the Nazis, and in what numbers. One thing seems to be clear: Hitler's military buildup was quite profitable for the owners of the large corporations. The big industrial corporation I. G. Farben, for example, which had close ties with the Nazi Party throughout its reign, built the slave-labor factory at Auschwitz, along with the gas used for mass killings (Broom and Shay 1992). Thyssen, Krupp, and Siemens, among many other large corporations, made huge profits from making war material.

The richest and oldest among the German capitalist families, however, were not overly supportive of Hitler, as indicated by Turner's (1985) extensive case study. As we consider further in the chapter on social stratification, some of the leading capitalists were among the early supporters of the Nazis: Fritz Thyssen of the huge Thyssen steel corporation was the most notable capitalist to back the Nazis before Hitler came to power (Broom and Shay 1992:9). Others such as Hermann Werner von Siemens of the Siemens conglomerate were consistent if not enthusiastic followers of Nazism throughout. Besides such business leaders as Flick, Thyssen, Borsig, and Kirdorf, many small entrepreneurs gave money to the Nazi Party to finance its election campaigns. But most who supported Nazism at the beginning were less supportive by the time war broke out. For example, Carl Bosch of I. G. Farben—and the nephew of Robert Bosch, the more famous founder of the Bosch Corporation (and something of a "socialist" in the late 1800s)—turned against Hitler. After personally warning Hitler of the danger he was bringing to Germany, Carl Bosch retired from his corporate position in 1935. Fritz Thyssen went further in rejecting Nazism and fled Germany in 1939, only to be

TABLE 2-1

Comparative Income Changes among the Rich,
1920s–1930s

Country	Percent Change for Richest 5 Percent
United Kingdom (1929–38)	-6%
United States (1929–41)	-20
Sweden (1930–35)	-7
Denmark (1925–39)	-6
Germany (1928–36)	+15

Source: Chirot (1986:163).

caught by the Nazis in France and sent back to a concentration camp in Germany for the remainder of the war (Turner 1985:339; Broom and Shay 1992:11).

It is interesting to note that in other industrial nations the gap between the rich and the poor was being reduced by liberal reform responses to the worldwide depression of the 1930s, as shown in Table 2–1. In Germany, however, under the Nazis the gap between rich capitalists and the working class increased considerably. In other words, what Table 2–1 shows is that the share of the overall income "pie" going to the rich went up in Germany while it was going down in the other major industrial nations (Chirot 1986:160–63). The outcome is rather predictable and in part related to a defining principle of fascism we noted above: a totalitarian movement based on nationalism that favors the elites, sometimes with a secondary element of racism.

GERMAN RECOVERY AND THE POSTWAR "ECONOMIC MIRACLE"

At the end of World War II, the allied powers—the United States, England, France, and the Soviet Union—divided Germany into four occupation zones. The plan was that all four powers would cooperate in reforming Germany and reconstructing the country after massive war damage. Part of the plan did not succeed, of course, because the Soviets wanted Germany to be a communist country, instrumental in the creation of a Soviet world empire. In short, the Soviets manipulated a new government in their sector of Germany and had this new government ask for Soviet tanks to shield the government when revolts broke out. This resulted in an East German satellite government for the old Soviet Union. What the East Germans thought of this communist government was expressed in June 1953 when many of them were killed by Soviet tanks in the streets of East Berlin, and also from 1949–61, when, on average,

200,000 left each year for West Germany before the Berlin Wall went up to stop them. In total, from the closing months of World War II in 1945 until 1961, some 15 million Germans fled or were expelled from their home in the former eastern provinces, including East Germany; an estimated 1 million also died while fleeing at the end of the war (Ardagh 1987:14). This massive migration confronted the young Federal Republic of Germany (West Germany) with one of the greatest tasks of social integration ever undertaken by a society in such a short period of time.

In the western, northern, and southern sections of Germany controlled by the US, British, and French, a massive restructuring of the political and economic system was under way in order to bring economic recovery and make future wars less likely. To a large extent, it was the United States that led the Allies in this re-forming of Germany, and retained control until 1955. Many of these reforms such as the new constitution, the Basic Law (Grundgesetz), were put in place by German politicians such as Konrad Adenauer, who had opposed Hitler before and during the war.

The "Economic Miracle"

At this point we should summarize some details of the post–World War II economic recovery of West Germany, or what has been called the "economic miracle" (Wirtschaftswunder).

One of the key reasons for Germany's rapid economic recovery was the **Marshall Plan,** named after the former head of the US State Department, George C. Marshall, who set up and administered this large-scale aid program starting in 1948 and limited to political allies of the United States. Knowing that an economic crisis, caused in large part by punishments against Germany after World War I, had fueled the rise of Hitler, this time the United States poured millions of dollars into Germany for rebuilding the economy and feeding its people. An equally strong motive for the Marshall Plan, though, involved the emerging Cold War with the Soviet Union: Soon after the end of World War II, the Cold War with the Soviet Union had already started and it was clear that a strong German economy was one of the best ways to stop Soviet expansion (Mosley 1978).

It was not just or even primarily US dollars that caused the economic miracle, however. Among the most important factors were new machinery and factories and skilled leaders such as Konrad Adenauer, mayor of Cologne before the war, and economist Ludwig Erhard. And as we will see in more detail later, the reduction in inequality within Germany soon after the war contributed extensively to economic growth and social peace (Hoffmeister and Tubach 1992:99). Perhaps more than anything, however, it was the unprecedented cooperation between labor and management in German companies that created the basis for economic expansion. To a greater extent than in any country previously, as we discuss later, management and workers cooperated in planning, making sacrifices, and working hard for Germany's economic recovery (Weber 1991:325). By the early 1950s the German economy was back to its pre-war level, and by 1964 the economy had tripled in size.

EAST GERMANY AND THE FALL OF THE WALL

Finally, in our brief summary of German history we must provide some basic information on what happened to East Germany, which was called the **German Democratic Republic** (GDR). We have seen that East Germany was created by and for the old Soviet Union. The East German communist government lasted until 1989, when the Berlin Wall came down—and its protectors with it. We know why East Germany was created in the early stages of the Cold War, but why did it fall, and seemingly so fast, which none of the experts, including social scientists, predicted?

The fall of East Germany can be understood only in light of the decline of the Soviet Union during the 1970s and 1980s. Simply, it can be said that the old Soviet Union was trying to build a world empire, but overextended itself with an economy that could not support this. As historical research following the modern world system model has shows, since about 500 years ago when economic competition increasingly became important for a country to remain a powerful nation in the world, attempts to create empires primarily through military power will not succeed in the long run (Chirot 1977; 1986; Wallerstein 1974, 1980, 1989).

For a few decades, of course, the Soviet Union did make spectacular strides toward economic modernization. According to Barrington Moore's class analysis noted earlier for the development of fascism, after the Russian Revolution of 1917, a communist state became possible in Russia largely because of the absence of a strong capitalist class, middle class, or working class to push for democracy (Moore 1966). Once established, **forced industrialization** (or industrialization achieved through making employees work long hours for very low pay, and with a focus on heavy industry rather than the production of consumer goods) became necessary for the state's survival in the face of foreign and internal threats against the communist state (Skocpol 1976, 1979:215). With Stalin's forced industrialization, beginning in the late 1920s, the Soviet Union did achieve rapid expansion of its industrial production to the point where it was second only to the United States in gross national product in the early years of the Cold War (1950–60).

By the early 1990s, however, the Soviet Union had collapsed, amazingly enough, to bring an end to the Cold War. The timing of the collapse was predicted by no one. But with hindsight we can see that the fall of the Soviet Union was not such a strange event in the modern world system after all.

Much like France in its wars and economic competition against the British during the 1700s, the Soviet economy was weakened due to military competition with the United States. The Dutch, British, and Americans, who, in turn, all had dominant positions in the modern world system in the last 400 years, all had comparatively small military budgets when they were rising to dominance. Military power came later (Kennedy 1987). The Soviets, on the other hand, tried to achieve dominance in the modern world system through military might, without first achieving the economic base to do so.

The "house of cards" that once was the Soviet bloc in Eastern Europe fell as well. From the study of **social movements, revolutions,** and **political violence,** we know that these events do not occur only because people have become angry and no longer accept oppression. Resource mobilization theory (McCarthy and Zald 1977; Kerbo 1982) tells us, for example, that rebellions and revolutions usually become massive events and are successful due to changes in the balance of power between the rebels and political authorities.

In 1953, 1956, and 1968, major rebellions developed in East Germany, Poland, Hungary, and finally Czechoslovakia. To end these rebellions against communism and Soviet dominance, Soviet tanks came in to crush the protests. In 1981, in the face of rebellion and the growing strength of the Solidarity movement in Poland, the Polish army itself stopped the movement and put leaders such as Lech Walesa in jail so that Soviet tanks would not return.

Much had changed in the Soviet Union before the next round of Eastern European rebellion occurred. By the late 1980s, the Solidarity movement in Poland was rising again. As Eastern Europeans waited in fear, and the whole world watched in amazement, the Soviet Union did not interfere. Rather, Mikhail Gorbachev, who had taken over as ruler of the Soviet Union in 1985, began to pull tanks out of Hungary in 1989. Within a year, the Berlin wall had fallen, and so had communist governments all over Eastern Europe. As in previous centuries of the modern world system, international competition among the core nations had led to the downfall of a major power.

Finally, as the GDR government fell, quite simply the eastern part of Germany joined the Federal Republic of Germany, which was established in the western part of Germany in 1949. The former East Germans elected their representatives to the West German government, and the constitution of West Germany was applied to the now united Germany. At the beginning of the newly united Germany there was celebration, with Beethoven's "Ode to Joy" from his Ninth Symphony played close to the site of the old wall and renamed for the occasion "Ode to Freedom." But the difficulties of unification with an economically backward East Germany soon set in, and will remain with Germany for another decade or two. This, however, is the subject for our final chapter on change in Germany today.

CONCLUSION

Among the most important aspects of German history that have shaped the present are Germany's late unification as a strong nation state and Germany's delayed economic development compared to most other states in Europe. Late development, as we see in more detail in our next chapter, created a very different kind of capitalism than found in the United States and many other industrial nations. And it was this late unification and economic development that can help us understand Germany's aggressive behavior in trying to gain new territories before World Wars I and II. As the British and others had done before them, the German elite believed they needed other countries to dominate and exploit for the greater development of modern Germany. And finally, though disastrously failing to expand their territories, the Germans were able to recover from World War II in one of the most impressive success stories of the world and German history.

We are now ready to take up the subject of modern Germany today, beginning with basic institutions. We begin with the German political system and the economy in Chapters 3 and 4, social stratification in Chapter 5, then move to the family, religion, and education in Chapters 6 and 7.

CHAPTER 3

The Political System

Recently, a book called *Little America: Die Amerikanisierung der Deutschen Republik* (Winter 1995) was on the best-seller list in Germany. As the title suggests, there was speculation that Germany is becoming a "little America," a prospect many Germans find quite unpleasant. While the United States is certainly respected by the great majority of Germans, they know all too well that the United States has far greater social problems than Germany, Americans work much longer hours for less pay, they read far fewer books, and young Americans with a high school education have a lower skill level than their German counterparts. Walking around the streets of German cities today gives one the impression that the American youth culture is becoming pervasive in Germany, and American products are certainly everywhere. And, of course, as we see in greater detail below, the sudden strength of the US economy and the sudden weakness of the German economy in the 1990s are putting pressure on Germany to copy some of the American corporate policies and how American universities are run.

Still, one does not find much of a change in the fundamental aspects of German society and culture toward a "little America." German institutions have been much more stable in the post–World War II period. Among the most basic institutions in all modern societies are the political system, economy, family, religion, and education. Sociologists define **institutions** as clusters of norms centered around important tasks in the society. Thus, as in other modern societies today, those examined in this chapter and the next are the most important in Germany. However, as the early masters of sociology have also shown us, while these institutions have become somewhat similar in all advanced industrial societies, historical traditions, cultural values, and even geography have worked together to create important differences in these major institutions in all modern societies.

Germany is no different in this respect. While in most ways the basic institutions of Germany today are closer to those of the United States than, for example, Japan, there are still significant differences. And many of these peculiarities stem from changes brought about in the post–World War II period. The old Federal Republic of Germany (West Germany) is regarded by most as "the winner of history." Germany has evolved from the greatest criminal of the 20th century to one of the most respected democracies in today's world. Germany is a world power again, though by way of economic achievement rather than military power.

In understanding Germany today we can suggest a rule of thumb, a rule certainly not universal in German institutions but useful: If Hitler liked it, most contemporary Germans reject it. Another rule, often cited at the time of the reunification in 1989–90, however, may not be quite as useful today: If Erich Honecker, the last leader of the communist GDR, liked it, most contemporary Germans reject it. A more complete explanation of this statement must wait until we cover more information about the "internal," not just the "formal," unification of the old East and West Germanies.

Most Americans would consider many conditions in modern Germany admirable, but others problematic. Among the admirable ones are a level of democracy not found in many nations, a level of equality and social security in striking contrast to that in the United States, and institutionalized labor–management cooperation envied by other capitalist nations. However, most Germans' rejection of the fascist hatred of other nationalities and races has created, until recently, the world's most liberal immigration and asylum laws. This resulted in a flood of immigrants at the end of the Cold War, creating much anxiety because immigrants were also granted thousands of dollars in welfare benefits each year.

This chapter provides a basic outline of the German political system. However, while it focuses on the most important characteristics of the German political system, it also notes in some detail the similarities and contrasts to American institutions.

THE GERMAN POLITICAL SYSTEM

People all over the world like to complain about politics and politicians. Among the complaints are that politicians always seem slow to make decisions, they waste taxpayers' money, and they seldom tell the truth. Germans complain as loudly as Americans, though often about different aspects of the political system because of differing values and characteristics of their political institutions.

Taxes, of course, are a constant complaint, but even here there are instructive differences. The average German pays up to 50 percent of his or her income in taxes and social security compared to the 25–30 percent range for Americans. What become major political issues or scandals can tell us much about differing values. While Germans smile at the American public's concern over sex and politics, they battle for years over the question of whether the police should be allowed to spy in private homes with technological means in order to combat organized crime. Differing expectations about what government should do, or what is defined as big government, are behind these differences, as we will see, especially in our section on the welfare state in Germany.

We should also be aware of the fact that German politics systematically attempt to come to terms with the traumatic experiences of this "extreme century," as Eric Hobsbawn called it. The failure of the Weimar Republic, National Socialism, World War II, the loss of land and people in the East, and the communist fate of East Germany have left a permanent imprint on the collective memory of Germans. Present institutions, most vividly the principles of German democracy, must therefore also be understood as reactions to the political failures of the 20th century.

Finally, in beginning this chapter it is important to note that in September 1998 the German voters pushed German politics into a new direction by sending the Social Democratic Party into power with a coalition with the leftist Green Party in what is called a "red-green alliance." The new German **chancellor**, Gerhard Schroeder, had the difficult task of trying to revive the German economy and reduce Germany's high unemployment rate of well above 10 percent as he took office in the fall of 1998. And while doing so, Mr. Schroeder has reversed some of the pro-business tax cuts and welfare cuts made by the previous chancellor, Helmut Kohl, who dominated German politics longer than anyone since World War II during 16 years as chancellor from 1982 to 1998. The next few years of German politics will, to say the least, be very important for the future of Germany.

In what follows in this chapter, along with the basic characteristics of the German political system, there are three major themes: Germany has established an intricate web of democratic institutions today, the German government has much more influence over what happens in most Germans' lives compared to the United States government, and, related to this, Germany has a very extensive welfare state compared to the United States. First, however, let's get to the basic principles.

The Democratic Institutions

As we have seen, Germany became a unified country for the first time in 1871, but the current political system of the **Federal Republic of Germany** is founded on the **Basic Law,** the German constitution instituted on May 23, 1949. Somewhat like Japan after World War II, but to a lesser extent, Germany had basic reforms imposed upon it by the Allied victors. Unlike Japan, however, which had her new constitution written by the American occupation forces under General MacArthur, German politicians who had opposed Hitler and Nazism (and in many cases fought against Hitler in the underground) were responsible for their new constitution.

With Berlin again becoming the capital city of the united Germany, there is a building boom in Berlin today. Many new government office buildings are under construction, while the remaining old office buildings of the communist era (such as the white one in the center of the photo) are being torn down or renovated for the new German government. The move presents many ironies, for example, the leader of the Green Party, Joschka Fischer, Foreign Minister of Germany, will occupy the old office of the hated communist dictator, Erich Honecker. Noting the irony, Mr. Fischer states, "we will deal with our history." One way Germans are "dealing with their history" is found in the old Reichstag building, the old German Parliament also used by Hitler's government. As the building is being remodeled for the new government in 1999, a false wall has been removed which covered negative graffiti written by American and Soviet soldiers against the Nazis soon after these soldiers captured Berlin, ending World War II in Germany and the Nazis's rule. For now the graffiti will be kept visible for all to see as they walk down the halls of the new capital building.

According to the Basic Law, Germany has what can best be described as a tripartite system of division of political power: legislative, judicial, and executive power. The legislative power is based upon a **parliamentary system** in contrast to the U.S. presidential system of government. This is to say that the people of Germany elect members to their legislature, the **Bundestag,** which, in turn, elects the head of government, the federal **chancellor** (Bundeskanzler). The chancellor not only appoints his ministers, but also determines the direction of his cabinet's policies. The federal government is therefore in the center of power emerging from the parliamentary majority.

As in a parliamentary system, normally the political party with the majority of seats in the *Bundestag* (or a coalition of parties if no one party has the absolute majority) elects their party leader to be chancellor.[2] Before September 1998, the Christian Democrats had a majority, in a coalition with the Free Democrats, with Helmut Kohl serving as chancellor since October 1982.[3] In September 1998, however, Chancellor Kohl's party was finally voted out of office. A new government was formed by the head of the Social Democratic Party, Gerhard Schroeder, who became chancellor in a coalition government in alliance with the Green Party.

The German political system also has a **federal president** as chief of state and first representative to the outside world, but this position is mostly of a symbolic nature (Mann 1992:986). The Basic Law attributes real power to the political parties and the chancellor who has the so-called guideline power. The Federal Republic of Germany has, therefore, been described as both a party state and a chancellor democracy.

Here again the negative experience with Hitler prompted the authors of the Basic Law not to favor a strong presidency although the president in the Weimar Republic had not been head of government at the same time. However, it had permitted President Hindenburg to bring Hitler to power, on the one hand, and Hitler to make laws and change the constitution without the consent of the parliament. The Basic Law is therefore based upon the idea of a president as a representative of the country, of the chancellor being elected by the parliament, a strong Federal Constitutional Court, a federal structure, and a clear division of power. While the constitution of the Weimar Republic had been based upon unity and freedom in that, for example, the labor leaders wrested the eight-hour day and the codetermination from the entrepreneurs, the temporary Basic Law of the Federal Republic could only focus on freedom, with unity being still far away.

In the context of Europe, it is also important to recognize that Germany has a **federal system** of government. This means that the individual states, or what Germans call **Laender,** have more political authority to run their own governments and make state laws, much like states in the United States. And much like the United States Senate *before* the 17th Amendment to the US Constitution in 1913, the 16 states[4] in Germany appoint members to a second legislative branch, the Federal Council or **Bundesrat,** which must approve part of the national legislation. These states have their own governments and are autonomous, for example, in the area of culture, education, and science.

Finally, in addition to the legislative branch of the federal government made up of the Bundestag and the Bundesrat, and the executive branch formed by the chancellor and his cabinet, there is a **judicial branch** with the Federal Constitutional Court at its top, in many respects like the US Supreme Court, and courts on the state and district levels.

As a complicating factor to what must be written about Germany today, soon after World War II, Germany was divided into what were popularly called East Germany and West Germany. The eastern part was dominated by the Communist Party put in place by the old Soviet Union in October 1949. The German Democratic Republic (GDR), however, dissolved with the crumbling of the Berlin Wall in 1989, and Germany was formally unified again on October 3, 1990. It is important to realize that there was no merging of the two political systems. Rather, the GDR simply disappeared by extending the West German Basic Law to former East Germany; that is, the latter joined the Federal Republic of Germany.

The German Government Bureaucracy

Without one further aspect, the German **government ministry,** or bureaucracy, the above description seems to suggest that the German system of government is quite close to that of the United States. What must be added, however, is that government bureaucrats, unelected career civil servants, placed in all offices on the federal, state, and community levels of public administration, have much more influence over government than is the case in the United States. In this respect, Germany is like most other governments of Europe and advanced nations in Asia, such as Japan. It is the United States that is unique (Dietrich 1991:277–84). Along with leading politicians in the political parties and the cabinet, these ministerial servants make up the core of the political class in Germany (Dahrendorf 1979).

At the top of each ministry—the Finance Ministry, the Justice Ministry, or the Foreign Ministry on the federal level—there is a political appointee, the minister (much like a member of the US president's cabinet), and in many cases one or two deputies (*Staatssekretaer*). However, below the minister there are many more career bureaucrats (*Beamte*) who often wield much more power than the average elected politician. This is true for each of the separate states in Germany as well. Much like in Japan (Kerbo and McKinstry 1995), these are the people who have extensive influence over government policy, are independent of electoral influence, and, in a way, actually run the German government.

While one may be critical of such a system, one must recognize that in contrast to the United States, where elected officials have almost exclusive power over legislation and government policy, these unelected ministry bureaucrats are not as motivated by "money politics" and lobbyists offering huge amounts of money to help their reelection. Those near the top of each ministry are career civil servants who have been doing their job for many years, in contrast to elected politicians who may hold office only briefly. This is also the main reason why they have the status of civil servant whose tenure makes them practically unremovable but also independent of political tides. Civil servants in Germany epitomize trust and continuity and are, therefore, crucial for political stability of Germany today.

Political Parties

There is no important political decision in Germany that does not go through the party machines. These decisions are prepared and taken by the parties but usually refined and translated into laws and regulations by the bureaucrats. According to the Basic Law, the parties—much more so in Germany than in the United States—serve as links between the political system and society. This is in large part because of a multiparty system stimulated by a parliamentary system rather than the US two-party presidential system. These parties in Germany represent the pluralism of opinions, interest groups facilitate discourse, and bring citizens into the political debate to a larger degree than most democratic societies, including the United States (Sontheimer 1973:95).

The two most important parties of the Federal Republic are the Christian Democratic Union (CDU), closely affiliated with its Bavarian sister, the Christian Social Union (CSU), and the Social Democrats (SPD). The Christian Democrats are no longer associated with religion in a strict sense, and neither are the Social Democrats a socialist workers' party. Together with the Free Democrats (FDP), the Christian Democrats may be located in the center and right of center of the political range, while the Social Democrats are left of the center. The leftist parties are the ecologically oriented *Die Grüenen/Buendnis 90* (Green Party) and the Party of Democratic Socialism (PDS), the successor of the former East German communist party (SED.)

Undoubtedly, the Christian Democrats are the party with the most governmental experience, as they have led German governments between 1949 and 1969, and again between 1982 and 1998. Much depended on their party leaders and chancellor candidates. Konrad Adenauer was the first chancellor and one of the founding fathers of the Federal Republic, while his political grandson, Helmut Kohl, was called the *eternal chancellor* because of his 16 years as chancellor. Both of them were masters in controlling the party and the rank and file politicians within their party.

The major successes of the CDU are also closely connected with the names of Adenauer and Kohl: integration into the Western alliance and joining **NATO** (North Atlantic Treaty Organization) after World War II, the rise of West Germany to an international economic power with its social market economy, monetary stability, the generation contract (pension and nursing care insurance), German reunification after the fall of the Berlin Wall, and European integration, which is still in progress. Therefore, it did not come as a surprise that the CDU won national elections with comfortable margins again in 1990 and 1994.

With persistently high unemployment, and simply a lack of new ideas among the leaders of the Christian Democrats, they were finally voted out in the fall of 1998. The Social Democrats, with their young star, Gerhard Schroeder, as the new chancellor took over the government in a red-green alliance with the Green Party. The Social Democratic Party is the oldest German party with roots as a workers' party dating back to the 19th century. As the first German party, the Social Democrats took over governmental responsibility in 1919, though they failed due to the constitutional weaknesses of the Weimar Republic and the absence of a democratic culture in Germany. During the 1970s and up to 1982, there were two internationally respected SPD chancellors, Willy Brandt and Helmut Schmidt, but the CDU dominated under Kohl for 16 years afterward.

The newest political party in Germany, and now the coalition partner in the new Social Democratic–led German government, the Green Party *(Die Grüenen)* freshened up the party landscape in the late 70s by orienting its goals against the political establishment. They demand alternative energies to fight pollution, reject atomic energy, and push for ecologically oriented production and tax systems. With respect to foreign affairs, many in the party favor leaving NATO and abolishing the Bundeswehr (military). The "green chaots," as they have been called, won 27 seats in the 1983 election to the 10th Bundestag. In recent years, however, the Greens have adapted more to German traditions. They no longer wear sweaters, jeans, and gym shoes in the parliament. Their leader and foreign minister as of 1998, Joschka Fischer, is now even for foreign engagement of the Bundeswehr, and the endorsement of NATO is just a matter of time. It was clearly the moderation of these policies by the Green Party that helped them win over 6 percent of the vote in the national elections of September 1998, allowing them to add their seats in the Bundestag to that of the Social Democratic Party and form a majority government. In coming months and years, however, a major question will be the ability of the moderate leadership of the Green Party to hold their more radical members in line to keep the red-green alliance from falling apart.

Finally, we should also consider the Party of Democratic Socialism (PDS) which succeeded the former GDR communist party and has kept about 300,000 members of the original 1.8 million. Many of them are still communist hardliners of GDR times. For the most part, however, the PDS is practically a regional party that profits from the disappointment of many East Germans with the German reunion and its aftermath. The party holds 36 seats in the Bundestag as of 1998 (Mertes 1996:304–7).

The Welfare State and Big Government

The first chapter noted that Germans seem to love rules. There are rules on everything, from when the grass may be cut, when showers are not permitted, to the size of garbage cans and hedges. A huge government bureaucracy is needed to write and administer all of these regulations and enforce them. Generally, of course, the more rules, the bigger the bureaucracy and the greater the need for it.

To be more accurate though, it is not simply the German preference for law, rules, and order that lead to big government. And we must stress that Germany's government is not much bigger than those of almost all other modern nations when compared to the much higher levels of government spending and government regulations in the other industrial nations.

There are many ways to measure government size and function. One typical measure is how much money is spent by the government as a percentage of the country's gross domestic product (GDP) or of the

TABLE 3–1

Government Spending as Percent of GDP, 1995

Country	Spending (as Percent of GDP)
Sweden	66.4%
Denmark	61.1
Finland	56.3
Belgium	53.3
Netherlands	52.8
France	50.9
Italy	49.5
Austria	47.8
Germany	**46.7**
Spain	42.6
England	42.3
Australia	36.2
Switzerland	36.7
United States	**35.8**
Japan	27.0

Source: Organization of Economic Cooperation and Development, http://www.oecd.org/puma/stats/govexp.htm.

total wages and profits generated within the country. As Table 3–1 shows, Germany is not very different from most European countries, and certainly does not have the biggest government. It is the United States that is quite atypical. As Table 3–2 shows, opinion polls find that Europeans prefer big government; that is, they prefer the governmental sector to be active in providing many services and dealing with many problems that Americans either ignore, simply tolerate, or have solved through private agents.

It is true that Germans, along with other Europeans, complain about taxes and about what government should be doing and is not doing, but they do not complain about big government in the same sense as Americans do. In fact, as the European unification is progressing, the nations with bigger governments in Europe are trying to make cuts in services to conform to the standards set by the European Union's executive headquarters in Brussels, Belgium, also called the European Commission. As these painful cuts take place, however, there have been and will continue to be massive protest in countries such as Germany and France. Their people tend to support big government and see the need for it.

There are several explanations of why the United States is so different from the rest of the advanced industrial nations on this subject, especially those in Europe (Lipset 1996; Ladd and Bowman 1998). To begin

TABLE 3-2

Comparative Attitudes Toward Inequality and Government Involvement in the Economy to Reduce Inequality

| | | | | | | | *Percent Answering Yes in* | | | |
Question	Hungary	Austria	Italy	West Germany	Switzerland	The Netherlands	Great Britain	Australia	United States
1. The government should provide everyone with a guaranteed basic income.	77.8	53.6	66.9	50.1	41.6	47.9	59.4	38.1	17.6
2. The government should provide a job for everyone who wants one.	90.0	76.9	82.0	74.3	48.4	73.8	57.9	39.7	44.0
3. The government should provide support for children from poor families to attend college.	71.6	78.3	89.8	84.8	80.7	84.1	82.6	74.0	75.2
4. It is the responsibility of government to reduce the differences in income between people with high incomes and those with low incomes.	76.9	76.7	81.0	55.9	41.1	63.9	62.9	43.8	28.3

Source: Simkus and Robert (1989); Kerbo (1996:260).

with, the American value system inherited primarily from England stresses individualism and small government. But the United States is even "further ahead" of the British with respect to these values. When the British sense of individualism came to the New World with its vast territory, this sense of individualism and independence expanded considerably. Also, the most individualistic Protestant religious sects immigrated to the new American territory, bringing an extreme sense of individualism to this country. Finally, it is very important to note that the United States is unique among the advanced industrial societies in never having experienced **feudalism,** that old form of societal organization that had pervaded the first world before industrialization. Feudalism was based upon cooperation and responsibility between landlord and peasant, the so-called *moral economy.* This was related to a sense of working together for mutual protection and survival. The feudal lord who owned the land generally had a sense of responsibility toward the peasants, and the peasants felt loyalty and obligation to the feudal lord. They exchanged military and social protection for loyalty and called it *fealty,* what we today call the *state.* It is this tradition that remains stronger in Europe and Asia and has never been present in the United States.

For Germans, there are more reasons for big government. First, we have already seen that the Prussian value system contained a more extreme form of this feudalism. Also, Germany was a late developing nation compared to others in Europe. Thus, Germany's experience with feudalism is much more recent, with an old landed aristocracy, the *Junker class,* holding exceptional influence well into the 20th century (Moore 1966; Bendix 1978; Kennedy 1987). All of these things have molded Germany's political institutions and individual consciousness, leading Germans to call for state interventions more often and, hence, to value government more than people in the United States.

The German Welfare State

It is difficult for Americans to imagine the extent of the welfare state and the resulting benefits in Germany today. Whenever news stories appear in major American newspapers on this topic, they *always* contain some editorializing statements to the effect that it will be impossible for Germany to continue on this path of big government and extensive welfare spending. The American mind-set simply cannot conceive of a capitalist nation surviving with such a welfare state. And while it may be true that the extent of the German welfare system has created problems for the economy in the 1990s, Germany has become the foremost economic power of Europe, and the third largest in the world, while this extensive welfare state was in place. It is time for more detail about what big government means in Germany.

Consider health care, for example. When Germans become ill they can look forward to perhaps the most extensive health care systems in the world. The system is based upon full coverage by insurance. As in most modern nations, the health care system in Germany is regulated and primarily funded by employers, employees, and the state (the United States is again the atypical country in this respect). Although hospitals, clinics, and physicians are independent from the government, the government regulates these health care providers as well as the public and private health insurance systems. With only a small user fee, all medical services are paid for by the national health care system. In Germany, practically everybody is covered by either the public or some form of private health insurance or both. People in the active labor force pay for it at 6.15 percent of their personal wages, while the employer also pays 6.15 percent. In addition, employer and employees equally share in financing the pension system (between 19 and 20 percent of wages), unemployment insurance (6.5 percent of wages), and old-age nursing insurance (1.7 percent).

By contrast, over 20 percent of Americans are not covered by either private or government medical insurance, and those who are covered by private medical insurance plans usually pay more for coverage than German citizens.

Germany, however, is even more extreme in the types of services that are covered compared to most other European countries. For example, until recently, every three years every citizen was entitled to four weeks of paid sick leave for treatments at a health spa (which is in addition to normal sick leaves no matter how often one is ill). With Chancellor Kohl's government cuts during 1997, however, Germans now get only three weeks of paid spa leave every four years, and must pay a small amount per day for it themselves. Before these changes, some 12 percent of the active labor force had gone on one of these sick leaves. During 1995, for example, these spa sick leaves cost the health insurance companies some $8 billion.

One other example of welfare benefits is worth mentioning: When Germans become unemployed, they at least have no worries of falling into poverty as do Americans. Depending on the length of previous employment and whether they are married and have children, unemployment benefits are paid for several years to those entitled and range from 53 to 67 percent of their net income when they were working. Welfare payments take over after that but go only to the needy based on 40 percent of the average net income of the population for a single person, plus an additional amount for other family members. With German wages the highest in the world (as we will see in more detail), Germans can do quite well materially on unemployment benefits.

As noted above, with the high level of benefits the German welfare state is under criticism. There have recently been, and will continue to be, cutbacks in the German welfare system. Thus, Germany, as many other European nations, is in search of a third way between the social-democratic type of welfare state and the "turbo-capitalism" of the United States. While the former has traditionally encouraged people to depend on the state to solve, for example, their labor market problems, the latter is geared toward getting people to help themselves in the first place. That is to say, the German labor market is a typical insider market: Job holders are well protected against unjustified layoffs, with the effect that people don't get easily unemployed. Once they do lose their job, however, they find it very difficult to get back into the labor market game again. Much the opposite is true in the United States, which is characterized by an outsider labor market. Since job incumbents can be fired more easily, Americans are on average more often unemployed but for a much shorter period of time than their German counterparts (Strasser 1997b).

An important point is that even with massive cuts, which are unlikely, the German welfare state, and that of most other European nations, will remain far larger than that of the United States.

EUROPEAN UNIFICATION

We cannot leave the subject of the German political system without discussion of the **European Union** (EU). For decades, many Europeans have envisioned a more unified group of nations in Europe with some common policies, laws, and military force. A few have even hoped for something like a United States of Europe to come to be before the year 2000. Steps toward a more unified Europe are finally coming into effect with the new EU. There is now a European Parliament of elected representatives from each member country, which meets in Strasbourg, France; as well as the European Commission (a kind of governing body with commissioners heading bureaucratic ministries) located in Brussels; a central bank (much like the US Federal Reserve) located in Frankfurt, Germany; and a European Court in Luxembourg.

The European Union is moving toward common policies in such areas as consumer and environmental protection, employee benefits, and support for "structurally underdeveloped regions," but it is still very far from a common foreign policy. Now every citizen from a member nation of the EU has a common passport and the freedom to live and work in any of the member nations (as does an American citizen who wishes to move from, say, New Mexico to New York). As of 1999 (and in 2002 with coins and bills), there will also be a common currency for member nations, the *Euro*. This development causes much anxiety among Germans as they fear not only losing the deutsche mark (DM) a symbol of a high standard of living but also the price stability connected with it—understandable after two inflations in this century caused people to lose their savings. In the words of the former head of the European Commission, the French Jacques Delors: "Other nations believe in God. The Germans believe in the deutsche mark." Indeed, by giving up the deutsche mark the Germans give up a piece of their identity as the DM symbolizes 50 years of social peace, stability, and prosperity.

As a consequence of a common currency, however, Americans traveling in Europe will, for the first time, be able to buy their Big Macs in Lulea in northern Sweden as easily as an original Italian pizza on the island of Sicily in the Mediterranean Sea. Introducing the Euro is not just having different coins in the pocket or in the cash register. It's a major step in the direction of not only economic but also political integration. In this sense, the introduction of the Euro may well be compared with the last all-European political project, the Westphalian Peace, which ended the Thirty Years War in 1648.

Increasingly, but only slowly and to a relatively small degree, Germany is therefore subject to a supranational level of governmental authority. It is too early to judge how far the authority of the EU will go, or the effects that will ensue. However, we are already seeing the need for countries in the EU to move toward some common policies, including foreign policy and government support for industry, as well as a revision of old policies such as the support of farmers. As economic logic would have it, the higher tax and higher welfare benefit countries such as Sweden and Germany must decrease both taxes and welfare benefits, otherwise the wealthy will leave Germany and the poorer Europeans will move into Germany given the free movement of member citizens. Higher prices for goods and services in these higher welfare countries will likely counter this movement of the poor, but only to some extent.

CONCLUSION

It is worth stating again that the German state is, comparatively speaking, much less unique than is that of the United States. The German state, its politicians, and its bureaucrats are more respected in Germany and tend to have more influence over what happens in all aspects of the society. Compared to Americans, Germans are much more supportive of big government and, on average, are also willing to pay high taxes for it. But as will be considered in more detail in Chapter 9, Germany will continue to change in the near future, particularly adapting to the changing world economy and defining a place in it. Government and people must adjust, and the adjustment will be difficult, as it means they must let go of many familiar comforts of life. These are the issues faced by the new Social Democratic government elected in the fall of 1998, issues that are most difficult to face. Even if the new Social Democratic government fails in its attempt to reverse the welfare cuts and lower taxes started by the previous Kohl government, Germany will still be a much different country in many respects than the United States.

The Economy

During the Cold War years, economic matters seemed easy for Americans to understand: Here was capitalism and there was communism. People in this part of the world seemed to feel sure they knew which was best, even if they thought that the old Soviet Union did not. The simplicity, however, crumbled with the Berlin wall. We must now recognize more than one *capitalism* on a global scale.

With no real threat from communism any longer, the anticommunist nations suddenly realized how many important economic conflicts they have with each other, and some very basic differences in economic philosophies as well. For the next several decades, world economic competition will likely become as intense as the old competition under the auspices of the Cold War, especially between the United States, Japan, and Europe (with Germany in a central position). The outcome of this economic competition will have a major impact on how Americans live and fare in the 21st century (Thurow 1991). After the relative economic decline of the United States in the 1970s and 1980s, the United States has recently regained the lead in many economic indicators. The long-term economic position of the United States, however, is far from certain. To understand all of this more fully, we must have a better grasp of how the world economy works, and the German economy is an important and intricate part of it.

There are four basic themes in this chapter: (1) The German economy is quite different from that of the United States in many ways. (2) The German economy has much more government involvement than the US economy. (3) There is considerably more worker/employee influence over aspects of company politics. (4) There is cooperation among major corporations in Germany that would likely be considered illegal in the United States. And, of course, we want to explain how all of these things affect the German economy and make it function differently than other economies. But first, there are again some basics to cover.

GERMAN CAPITALISM

Since Germany is a capitalist nation, its economy is based upon private ownership of the means of production (factories, machines, shops, etc.), and having private property is both an important personal goal and a significant status dimension. This definition also implies something of a free market system, without cartels of corporations removing competition, nor government intervention to do the same. However, all of these characteristics of capitalism can vary in degree.

We begin with the private ownership of the means of production. According to one basic measure, Germany is not the richest country in the world today. World Bank statistics for 1996, for example, show Germany is only ranked sixth with $28,870 per capita gross income, with Switzerland taking the lead with $44,350, and the United States in eighth place with $28,020 (*Die Welt*, October 30, 1998). However, there are certainly wealthy capitalists in Germany: In fact, as a percentage of population, there are more billionaires in Germany than in the United States— 5.1 per 10 million people in Germany versus 3.8 for the United States (Shapiro 1992; Kerbo 1996:490). Again, however, the number of rich people alone in Germany can be misleading. The most important source of ownership of the means of production today is corporate stock. Some 50 percent of American families own at least a small amount of corporate stock, and about 52 percent of all stock in US corporations is owned by people—with about 1 percent of the richest Americans owning over half of this privately held stock, though (Kerbo 1996). Most of the remaining US corporate stock is held by big pension funds and invested only for the long-term benefit of retirees.

In Germany, by contrast, less than 10 percent of the people own any corporate stock, and only 14 percent of all German corporate stock is owned by people. By at least one definition, what this suggests is that there are few real capitalists in Germany! In sharp divergence from the pattern in the United States, much of the German corporate stock is held by other corporations (some 42 percent of the total, with big banks leading the way), and about 10 percent is held by the federal, state, and local governments. For example, the federal government owns a substantial part of the stock of the national airline (Lufthansa), and even larger portions of the railroad and telephone system, which had been exclusively state owned and managed until very recently (Garten 1992). Also interesting is that one of the states, Lower Saxony, owns about 20 percent of Volkswagen, with state governments owning the so-called state banks and parts of other famous auto companies as well. Overall, the different levels of German government own more stock than does any other government in the world (Thurow 1991:36).

There is one further aspect of corporate ownership and corporate structure in Germany that requires explanation: the place of large German banks. To a far greater extent than in the United States, German banks—both private and state owned—own large amounts of corporate

TABLE 4−1

Examples of Corporate Ownership by German Banks

	Percent of Stock Owned by Bank		
Corporation	Percent	Corporation	Percent
Deutsche Bank			
Allianz	10%	Kloeckner, Humboldt, Deutz	41%
Muenchner Rueck	25	Linde	10
Daimler-Benz	25	Muenchner Rueck	10
Karstadt	10	Suedzucker	17
Philip Holzmann	26	Hapag-Lloyd	10
Dresdner Bank			
Allianz	10	Veba	5
Bilfinger & Berger	25	BMW	5
Hapag-Lloyd	10	Muenchner Rueck	10

Source: Data from Liedtke (1994).

stock in other corporations, giving them extensive influence over these corporations and their policies (Kerbo and McKinstry 1995).[5]

Let us consider the largest of the German banks, the Deutsche Bank. As shown in Table 4–1, this bank owns a significant amount of stock in some of the biggest German corporations. Dresdner Bank, traditionally the second largest German bank (although there are presently a number of mergers going on in the German bank scene), shows the same pattern. Japan is famous for its groupings of corporations, called *keiretsu*, that coordinate much of Japan's economy (Gerlach 1992; Abeggelen and Stalk 1985). We find a somewhat similar situation in Germany, but with what must be called **bank keiretsus,** in contrast to the Japanese case where large industrial corporations own as much of the stock in banks as the banks own of industrials (which means they own each other).

Combining all of the above—the influence of German governmental agencies over the economy discussed in the previous chapter, government ownership of stock, and the extensive bank domination of corporate stock, along with the relative lack of people owning corporate stock—we can hypothesize that the German government and big banks (alone or together) are much more able to control economic activity than found in the United States. Whether this "concerted" economy will be stronger and better able to survive in coming decades compared to the free-wheeling American economy, with little long-term planning and more deadly competition, is an extremely important issue. However, it is a question beyond the scope of this book.

GERMANY'S ECONOMIC DEVELOPMENT AFTER 1945

At the end of World War II Germany was in ruins. Almost all basic necessities were in short supply, and some 20 percent of the houses and factories were destroyed. In 1947, German industry still produced at less than a third of its pre-war level. The Allies controlling Germany right after the war tried to ease these hardships with food coupons for imported food, pay freezes, and price controls. Money became worthless with cigarettes taking the place of the old currency. However, in 1948, the economic reforms finally took effect, and the deutsche mark was introduced in the three Western zones (controlled by the Western Allies). By 1950, the economic output of West Germany had already exceeded that of 1936; and by the 1960s the German economy was growing at a much faster rate than almost all other economies in the world.

Undoubtedly, the "economic miracle" of the 50s and the 60s was facilitated by the extensive aid Germany received under the auspices of the Marshall Plan. But it is also clear that the new economic structure that emerged after World War II helped make this economic miracle possible. As we have seen, it was an economic structure that allowed more coordinated economic policies and social cooperation. And as we discuss below, it was a very different economic system: one that provided for extensive worker participation and influence in the economy. In this re-

The BMW head office in Munich (shaped like motor pistons) symbolizes the importance of the auto industry for the German economy. BMW started out as a maker of motorcycles, then small cars, and finally, like Mercedes-Benz (now Daimler-Chrysler after merging with the US company, Chrysler), BMW has taken much of the high end of the auto market in the world. Like many other industries, Germany has specialized in the higher quality products in world competition. For many, BMW symbolizes "made in Germany."

spect, the United States and Germany could not have been more different. The new German leaders strongly believed that capitalism *and* democracy, the growth of the (welfare) state *and* the (market) economy, would lead to the wealth of the nation and a higher standard of living for its members (Dettling 1986).

Meanwhile, the "other" Germany, the GDR (East Germany), followed the basic Soviet (communist) model of a planned economy in which the plan and not the market was the measuring rod of all things. If a society is run like a large-scale enterprise, those who manage the enterprise, the officials, have the power and distribute the privileges, that is, both power and economic rewards. In 1989, the year in which the Berlin wall came down, the level of GDR productivity was only 30 to 40 percent of that of West Germany. And those employed in the GDR received only one-third of the average West German income. Of course, the main reason for this economic stagnation was the lack of efficiency, innovative pressure, and individual motivation. For example, the industrial machines in the GDR were much older than in West Germany, and, while unemployment did officially not exist, the low level of productivity was tantamount to overemployment (Geissler 1996:53).

To be sure, the starting position of the GDR was not as good as that of the Federal Republic. Contrary to the relatively affluent Western Allies, the Soviet Union had been economically exhausted by the war. As the force that came to occupy East Germany, it subsequently exploited the GDR by buying underpriced commodities and dismantling factories. By 1953, for example, the East Germans had paid 60 times more reparations (war penalties) than the West Germans.

Life in East Germany was characterized by waiting in lines for everything and patience. Due to the centrally planned economy's inability to satisfy consumers' demand, certain products were only available from time to time, and other products such as cars only after waiting 10 or more years after ordering them. Just before the decline of the GDR in 1989, there were only 39 color TVs and 7 telephones for every 100 households, as compared to the Federal Republic with 86 and 92, respectively. Many East German jokes attacked these conditions, such as the one: "The real reason East Germany didn't have too many robberies in the old days was that you had to wait 18 years for a getaway car."

East Germans, on the other hand, enjoyed very cheap public transportation and cheap, though often run-down, housing. While the GDR media were engaged in a permanent campaign against the alleged social injustice and mass unemployment in the "imperialist West," West German TV programs, which could be received in most regions of the GDR, brought the overt differences in the standards of living between the two parts of Germany to light. In the long run, this caused discontent among East Germans, which was eventually expressed in peaceful demonstrations triggered by Gorbatchev's perestroika (openness in the Soviet Union). The stage was set for the collapse of the GDR in the fall of 1989.

After the fall of the Berlin Wall and the GDR government, the transformation of the old East German political and economic system affected practically every aspect of life in the East. The initial euphoria accompanying the reunification in both the East and West was soon forgotten with mounting problems. The government had misjudged the situation when it thought the costs of reunification could be taken care of without raising taxes. With the breakup of the Soviet Union, the communist states of Eastern Europe collapsed practically overnight, hence almost eliminating the traditional market for East German products. At about the same time, in 1991, the European Union emerged from the European Community. It became a single market in 1993 and added three new member states in 1995, for a total of 15. These changes in Europe resulted in increased competition for East German firms.

Thus, East German industrial production dropped between 1989 and 1993 to 30 percent of what it was before (Fuerstenberg 1995). Many state-owned companies had to be closed and thousands of workers laid off. In many regions of the former GDR, roads, railway networks, and telecommunications had to be renewed, which meant that in 1996 almost half of the former East Germany's gross national product was transferred from West Germany. By 1995, these transfer payments had reached well over 1 trillion deutsche mark (Schewe 1996:223; Hettlage and Lenz 1995). The eastern part of Germany today is making slow progress in reindustrializing. There is still a long way to go, and it has been much more difficult than anyone believed when the Berlin Wall came down in 1989 and Chancellor Kohl spoke of the "blooming regions" to become reality within a few years.

WORKING IN GERMANY AND WORKER INFLUENCE

It is time to return to one aspect of the new German economy after World War II that helped set the stage for the economic miracle. It is worth stating again that it is quite likely that no other country in the world has better conditions and benefits for employees today. Germany has in fact been referred to as a producer- and employee-centered nation in contrast to the consumer-centered United States.

We have already seen that health and welfare benefits are extensive. Consider also that German employees have the highest pay of all industrial nations and work fewer hours annually than the workers of any other country, as shown in Table 4–2. The average workweek in Germany is close to 35 hours. German employees are legally entitled to 4 to 6 weeks of paid vacation time each year, as well as a generous amount of national holidays and extra paid leaves for such things as continuing education, and unpaid leaves for rearing children. (Germans like to point out that it is fortunate that about half the population is Catholic and half Protestant so they can have all of the holidays of both.)

TABLE 4–2

Comparative Labor Costs and Working Hours, 1994

Country	Manufacturing Wages per Hour (including benefits)	Average Hours Worked per Year
West Germany	$30.32	1,620
Switzerland	28.60	1,838
Belgium	25.76	1,729
Norway	25.06	1,740
Japan	24.83	1,880
Austria	24.27	1,722
Netherlands	24.05	1,714
Denmark	23.73	1,687
Sweden	21.38	1,824
France	19.94	1,755
USA	19.29	1,896
Italy	18.76	1,744
East Germany	18.29	1,737
Ireland	15.28	1,794
Britain	15.21	1,752
Spain	13.96	1,772
Greece	8.41	1,832
Portugal	6.32	1,882

Sources: Institute for the German Economy; and *Los Angeles Times,* February 25, 1996.

The concept of a producer- and employee-oriented nation comes also from the focus on convenience for workers as opposed to service for consumers. By law in Germany, almost all shops—including food markets, clothing and department stores, and bakeries—had to close until recently by 1 or 2 PM on Saturdays (it's now by 4 PM) and remain closed until Monday morning. During the week stores must close by 6 PM (except Thursday evenings by 8 PM). Many small shops also take a midday break from about 1 until 3 PM. Innumerous foreign visitors not being aware of these rules and arriving on a Saturday afternoon have found themselves without food in the house. The only exceptions are restaurants, only recently bakeries on Sundays from 10 AM to 12 PM, and small food shops in train stations and airports. However, further liberalization of the opening laws is probably only a matter of time. (At the present time, then, one can understand a predominance of German license plates on the cars parked at shopping centers in the Dutch towns close to the German border on weekends.)

It is not simply, however, that German employees are offered many types of benefits, protection, and conveniences, but also that they have considerable influence in the workplace. As we see in more detail in the next chapter, by law every shop, factory, or office with more than five employees must give these employees the right to elect a **works council** (Thelen 1991; Turner 1991). The greater the number of employees in the establishment, the larger the membership of the works council.

The most important part of this so-called **codetermination law,** and the part that would likely give American employers heart attacks, pertains to the influence of these organized workers: Almost all management decisions—from hiring and firing employees to changes in working hours, working conditions, and the introduction of new machinery—*must be approved* by the works council. Moreover, management must open the books to works council members: Workers have the right to inspect all documents and account sheets to obtain knowledge of how the company is doing financially in order to make intelligent decisions about proposed management policies.

In addition to all of this, almost every company and government agency in Germany has union representation. In what is often called a **dual system,** German workers are then represented by the works council representatives and by a union (Thelen 1991; Turner 1991). As the system has evolved since World War II, the works councils take care of matters on each shop floor or office, while the unions focus on workers' interests on broader, industrywide or national issues.

Finally, by German law, about half of all corporate board members must be regular employees of the corporation, elected by the employees of the corporation. The corporate board of directors (as it is called in the United States), of course, is the place where major long-term policies are decided, as well as the hiring and firing of top management. Thus, from top to bottom, in German corporations workers are well represented and have a fairly high degree of influence in the corporation or government work place.

Outcomes of German Worker Influence

Reasons for the remarkable position and influence of German workers will be taken up in our next chapter on social stratification. At this point, however, some of the economic outcomes of worker influence in Germany are important to consider. As might be expected with German economic problems in the second half of the 1990s, there is much criticism of the power and position of German employees. Whether the positive outcomes outweigh the negative over the long term is one of the most important questions for the future of management–employee relations and work organization in Germany as well as in all other capitalist countries, as we consider in our final chapter. We begin our discussion of outcomes of worker influence by first considering the negative consequences that have received considerable press coverage in the United States. Then we turn to some of the important positive outcomes.

It is not difficult to understand that with the highest wages and benefits in the world, and with the shortest working hours, German employees are quite expensive and increase the prices of German products and services. Further, when workers have so much influence through unions and works councils, it is difficult for management to lay off employees, introduce new machinery, change work organization, or do many other things that will allow the company to rapidly adjust to market requirements. Also, it is said, companies are quite reluctant to hire new employees when they will be so expensive and difficult to lay off if no longer needed. Hence, many German companies resort to considerable overtime work, thus preventing new jobs and keeping the German unemployment rate high. Such countries as Ireland, New Zealand, and Australia have been able to increase the number of people in the active labor force by more than 10 percent between 1993 and 1997, while Germany lost 5.3 percent. According to a recent study presented at the World Economic Forum in Geneva, the German economy was only ranked 24th out of 53 countries in a comparison of their competitive potential measured in terms of unemployment, labor market flexibility, and taxes; the United States came in 3rd behind Singapore and Hong Kong (*Die Welt,* June 5, 1998).

With so many negative outcomes of worker power and influence in Germany cited by management and the mass media in recent years, one wonders how Germany came to be the third largest economy in the world and by far the strongest in Europe. There are, in fact, many *positive benefits* of extensive worker influence in German companies, which are usually overlooked in the US media—positive benefits that even most German managers concede (Thelen 1991).

We begin by simply noting what sociologists have long explained: the greater the commitment members of any organization have to that organization, the more they will sacrifice and work hard for the benefit of that organization (Collins 1975; Lincoln and Kalleberg 1990). This is one of the basic outcomes of the German work laws that make German workers real members of the organization, and not just expendable pieces of machinery. German employees are a part of the decision-making process. By law they are given the vital information from the company's balance sheets, and, because they are much more likely to be life-time employees of the corporation, they show greater loyalty and commitment.

German workers, of course, are not perfect. German public and private employees have in fact come under heavy attack in recent years for their lack of a service mentality. They are reproached for automatically receiving costly benefits without having to do something in return. Still, the lack of a service mentality is not the same as less commitment to the organization, and, when compared to workers in most other countries, we tend to find more committed employees in Germany.

There are also counterarguments to the other negative aspects of German labor conditions noted above. With respect to the high cost of German labor, there is evidence that because of their commitment and vocational training, German workers are among the most hardworking, productive, and dependable in the world. A few years ago when we were interviewing managers of Japanese corporations with operations in Germany, one Japanese manager in his broken English explained that while Germans have fewer working hours, "when they work it is beautiful!" (Kerbo, Wittenhagen, and Nakao 1994a;1994b).

To understand one of the major benefits of works councils and strong German unions, the individualistic orientation of workers in Western industrial nations has to be acknowledged. Western child rearing methods and Western culture will likely never allow the tendency toward identification with the company and the extent of cooperation with the work group found in Asian countries such as Japan. However, neither can all workers seek only their own interests without due regard for group needs if a particular company is to survive.[6]

There is another major outcome of codetermination laws in Germany that creates a major benefit for both employees and managers: When workers are given some voice in the decisions that affect their jobs and incomes, they feel more secure and more protected, and, therefore, are less likely to block change and new technology and less likely to go on strike. For example, between 1980 and 1989, West German employees were on strike 28 days on average, compared to their US counterparts 123 days; between 1990 and 1996 the figures are 17 and 44, respectively; and for 1996 only 42 strike days were counted (Institut der Deutschen Wirtschaft 1998:149). Moreover, workers in the United States are more likely to resist change and new technology than are German workers. American workers feel their jobs will be threatened.

Finally, a four-year ongoing study of the attitudes of German corporate executives toward the codetermination laws and works councils found that a majority of the executives supported these laws and works councils, and agreed they and their companies are better off because of them (Wever 1991). For example, most executives in this study agreed that works councils are (1) more practical and easier to work with than the highly ideological unions of the past, (2) often reduce tension between labor and management, (3) are more likely to get workers to go along with agreements, and (4) were helpful in times of change, especially in helping workers understand the need for change to protect profits and jobs. These German executives were also likely to say they were proud of the system of worker–manager relations, especially in contrast to what exists in the United States.

CONCLUSION

In closing we need to note again that these work laws, works councils, and strong unions in Germany have come under increasing criticism as the German economy lingers in recession during the second half of the 1990s. Changes are occurring. German managers are starting to wonder if the old ways can be continued in the face of American companies undercutting prices more and more because of much lower wages and benefits. Some health and welfare benefits were reduced in the final months of the Kohl government in 1998; for example, amendments to work laws were made so that it is easier to fire workers in very small companies. However, the new Social Democratic–Green coalition government has reversed most of these changes as they pledged to.

Whether the American economy with very little union representation and almost no worker input on the shop floor, and thus low wages and easy layoffs, will continue to outperform the German economy, or old–style German productivity and innovation with highly committed and skilled workers will make a comeback, remains a crucial question for the future of work organization of all capitalist countries. Thus, the frame of economic competition for the 21st century has been set. We turn to other details of social structures that set the stage for the new economic competition in our next chapter on social stratification in Germany today.

Social Stratification

New Forms of Inequality and Class Relations

Aspects of **social stratification** in Germany can be puzzling for Americans visiting the country for the first time. Things just don't seem to fit American assumptions. When traveling around Germany, it seems quite evident that there is much less material inequality and poverty than in the United States. There are simply fewer examples of a large gap between the rich and poor as seen so often in the United States. There are no slums or ghetto areas to speak of, which is especially curious considering the German unemployment rate of about 11 percent in the late 1990s. Yes, there are some homeless people in the big cities such as Frankfurt, Leipzig, and Berlin, but nothing like the levels of homelessness seen in the United States. While living and working in Germany a few years ago, the American author of this book was visited by relatives. After days of driving around showing them the sights, one asked, "So where do the poor people live?" They had seen about all it was possible to see and no poor people.

As we will consider in more detail, many kinds of statistics support these observations. We have already seen in previous chapters that there is a rather high level of democracy in post–World War II Germany, another form of relative equality. So why do such things not seem to fit with other impressions and observations about Germany?

Considerable insight into American society came from an early French visitor, Alexis de Tocqueville. After his visit in the 1830s, de Tocqueville (1969:9) wrote, "No novelty in the United States struck me more vividly during my stay there than the equality of conditions." Such words could well have been written by a German visiting the United States at the time. Compared to France and Germany in the 1800s (and ignoring the condition of slavery for many Americans), the United States *did* have greater equality of all kinds. What impressed de Tocqueville even more was the equality of treatment and respect people seemed to receive, an informality in social interactions, and a lack of status rituals given to people in positions of authority.

Many of the conditions in Europe and the United States have changed since de Tocqueville's time. With respect to post–World War II Germany, to be specific, the United States now has much more *material inequality*. But one aspect of our subject has changed much less: While the United States remains the nation of informal interactions, relatively uncolored by deference rituals given to higher status people by those of lower status, to a large extent Germany remains a country of widespread *status inequalities*. The United States, of course, never had a feudal system as did all European societies. There are no dukes or duchesses, princes or princesses found in the United States. But there is more to it than that. Everywhere in German society one finds deference given to people of accomplishment and/or authority; the language still requires more formality when speaking to people of higher status, and titles abound. As noted earlier, a visiting American professor, for example, may be taken back, and eventually amused, to perpetually hear "Herr or Frau Professor Doktor" before his or her name.

An important point, however, is that there is more than one dimension of ranking, inequality, or what we call *stratification* in a society. Since World War II, Germany has moved toward greater material and political equality, while material inequalities have become greater in the United States. But to a large degree, Germany has not lost the tendency of ranking people by some definition of status or prestige. It is this contrasting combination of equality and inequality that Americans may find somehow strange. Things look more equal in Germany, but at times ranking seems so important.

In this chapter we explore why these differences are found in Germany. We consider theories, as well as research, on the subject. We then move to the subjects of gender inequalities, the level of social mobility up and down the system of ranks, and, finally, the nature of a remaining upper class in Germany today. The subject of race and ethnic inequalities will be considered more fully in Chapter 8, "Social problems."

THE NATURE OF SOCIAL STRATIFICATION

By **social stratification** we mean a system of ranking within society, a system of ranking that has become well established and affects many things about how people live. There will always be some types of inequalities and a system of social stratification in all but the most simple societies (Kerbo 1996). However, the level of these inequalities, and which are most important in affecting how people live, varies greatly around the world and through history. We need to consider this subject further to understand why stratification systems such as those in Germany and the United States are different.

It is useful to begin an explanation of social stratification in Germany by using Max Weber's concepts of **class, status,** and **power** (or party). It was Weber who offered a multidimensional view of social stratification in his criticism of Marx's one-dimensional view based only on economics, which is to say, the ownership versus nonownership of the means of production (Gerth and Mills 1946:181–194; Kerbo 1996:102–104). In addition to Marx's economic dimension of stratification that divides people into different classes, Weber refers to the importance of economic divisions based upon the level of education and skill. Weber showed us how status ranking, or divisions based upon prestige and honor, along with divisions based upon power and authority in political and bureaucratic organizations in modern societies are also important, and at times more important in forming distinctive groups than economic stratification. Weber stressed that all three dimensions of stratification (class, status, and power) exist in a society, but that one or two of these dimensions will be more important, depending upon the kind of stratification system that exists in that society (Kerbo 1996:Chapter 4).

As should be evident from our opening description of equalities and inequalities in Germany compared to the United States, inequalities of class have become less important in Germany, while the status dimension of ranking remains more important. Given Germany's feudal traditions and Prussian values of order and authority described in earlier chapters, the importance of status ranking in Germany is not difficult to understand. It is the relative class and material equalities in Germany that require more explanation.

Reduced Inequality

Germany was certainly not always a land of relative material equality. In fact, before World War II, wealth and income inequalities were considerably greater (Kerbo 1996:Chapter 15). Much like Japan, many aspects of the German social structure have considerably changed after the old fortunes were more or less destroyed by war (Kerbo and McKinstry 1995, 1998). The rather remarkable "equalization of burdens law" (Lastenausgleichgesetz), which was enacted in 1952, helped start the trend toward less inequality in Germany. This law mandated a kind of burden sharing whereby taxes were used to reimburse those who had lost their property due to the war and the currency reform, especially the millions who fled from eastern parts of Germany. By 1982, when the last payments were made under this law, over 121 billion DM had been redistributed (Ardagh 1987:15; Hoffmeister and Tubach 1992:105; von Beyme 1984:89).

To a small extent, the postwar breakup of some of the large corporations by the new German government (with Western Allies' backing) helped reduce inequality (Spohn and Bodemann 1989). However, more important in the process of reducing income inequality were labor laws and increasingly strong labor unions, noted in the previous chapter and of which we have more to say.

T A B L E   5–1

The Reduction of Income Inequality in Postwar
West Germany

	1950	1960	1970	1981	1985
Gini coefficient	.396	.380	.392	.347	.344
Shares of income:					
Bottom 20%	5.4	6.0	5.9	7.2	7.4
Top 20%	45.2	43.9	45.6	42.4	43.0
	1963	**1969**	**1973**	**1978**	**1983**
Percent in poverty (40% of median income)	5.7%	2.7%	1.4%	1.6%	2.0%

Source: Glatzer et al. (1992:209).

As a result of all this, when the German economy began to grow rapidly by the 1960s, the standard of living for the vast majority of West Germans improved and income inequality dropped, as indicated in Table 5–1. For example, in 1950 the bottom 20 percent of the population had 5.4 percent of the income while the top 20 percent of the population enjoyed over 45 percent of the income. By 1985, the bottom 20 percent of the population had 7.4 percent of the income, while the top 20 percent of the population had their share reduced to 43 percent of the income (Glatzer et al. 1992:205).[7] The same trend is reflected in the poverty rate for Germany from 1963 to 1983: There was a steady decline in poverty as measured by how many people were below 40 percent of the median income in each year (from 5.7 percent in 1963 to around 2.0 percent in 1983).

This measure of poverty is in fact a better indicator of the level of inequality than the poverty rate measured in the United States. It is worth noting that if poverty in the United States were defined as being 40 percent or less of the median income, through the 1980s as well as in the mid-1990s the equivalent poverty rate for the United States would be around 20.0 percent of the population compared to Germany's 2 to 5 percent (see, for example, Mishel and Bernstein 1993:277–80; Hanesch et al. 1994:138). Also as shown in Table 5–1, the Gini coefficient (a statistical measure of income inequality based upon the income shares of the population) dropped in the postwar period.

By the time the Berlin Wall came down in 1989, Germany, along with Japan, had one of the most equal income distributions of all advanced industrial societies, while the United States had the most unequal income distribution (Hanesch et al. 1994).

Before moving away from this brief historical description of inequality in Germany, we must note trends that are developing in the 1990s. In the unified Germany of the 1990s we observe wide income disparity between the formerly eastern and western sections of Germany, as well as an the economic slowdown largely related to the short-term costs of unification. As the eastern part of Germany is further rebuilt in coming years, the level of inequality between the East and West will no doubt be reduced. However, how much it will be reduced and how long it will take are important questions for the future of social stratification in Germany.

GERMAN WORKERS AND WAGES

It is time to consider another important reason for reduced inequality in post–World War II Germany. Based on our description in Chapter 4 of German corporations and the keiretsu-type corporate structures centered around large banks, one might assume that German workers have little influence in such a system. In contrast to the United States, however, such an assumption could not be further from the truth. We have already seen the overall figures on comparative income equality in Germany. Looking within corporations in Germany themselves is even more interesting for this subject. Across all large corporations in major industrial countries we find that the gap between the typical manufacturing worker's pay and the typical chief executive officer's is 11 to 1 in Japan and 10 to 1 in Germany, while it is highest in the United States with at least 25 to 1 or higher.[8] Other research comparing Germany, Japan, Canada, Italy, France, England, and the United States found the average manufacturing employee's income was highest in Germany, third highest in Japan, and lowest in the United States and England. The income of chief executive officers, however, was found to be highest in the United States ($717,237, almost double the pay of second place France), while executives in Germany and Japan were at the bottom with almost identical annual incomes of about $391,000 in 1991 dollars (Kerbo 1996:30; Mishel and Bernstein 1993:204).

The point is that German workers have few equals when it comes to wages and other benefits, short working hours, government protection, and many other conditions workers around the world can only look upon with envy. To put it crudely, the wealthy and corporate elites in Germany did not suddenly or for altruistic reasons decide to give workers a better deal. It is our task at present to provide some explanation why German workers are envied by most workers in the world. We must begin with a brief history of the Works Constitution Act, Codetermination Law, and other means of labor influence in Germany we considered briefly in the previous chapter. These constitute some of the most important differences between the systems of social stratification in Germany and the United States.

A HISTORY OF GERMAN LABOR LAWS

While conducting research on relations between Japanese managers and German employees in Japanese transplant corporations in Germany, we

asked German personnel managers to explain some of the problems associated with their jobs in Japanese corporations. In a common response,
one of our informants stated, "Japanese corporate executives here do not
think the position of personnel manager is such a complex job." He went
on to describe how the job of personnel manager in Germany involves
much more than hiring and firing of employees, especially because there
must be continuous and complex negotiations with employees on almost
every issue (Kerbo, Wittenhagen, and Nakao 1994a, 1994b; Lincoln,
Kerbo, and Wittenhagen 1995). Workers in Germany are not simply told
what policies they must follow. Indeed, because of labor laws, it can be
said that German workers have more rights and influence in what happens in the workplace, and often the company generally, than any other
workers in the world (see Thelen 1991 and Turner 1991). These labor laws
apply to any corporation with operations in Germany, whether the company is German, American, Swiss, French, Japanese, or of any other origin.

As mentioned above the term **dual system** is used to describe the
German form of labor representation that has evolved since World War II.
This dual system involves (1) legally mandated equal employee representation on the corporate board of directors, along with representation on
the shop floor level by "works councils," and (2) powerful labor unions
representing labor in issues beyond the individual plant level.

Soon after World War II, labor unions were able to regain strength
after having been destroyed by Hitler. By 1952, labor laws first pushed as
early as 1848 were finally enacted by the German government, giving
workers extensive rights and specific representation in each company,
above the very smallest. Workers have elected worker representatives on
corporate boards of directors and **works councils** (Hoffmeister and
Tubach 1992:180). Fearing the consequences of greater labor union influence after World War II, the conservative German government in the
1960s tried to weaken labor unions through laws intended to isolate
worker representatives in each corporation, creating something like
"company unions." The idea backfired, however, when labor unions in
fact did not decline in influence or worker support but learned to cooperate with works councils and worker board members in each corporation
for influence on two fronts, from within each company and from without
(Thelen 1991). With a more liberal government under Chancellor Willy
Brandt in the 1970s, these labor laws were expanded in 1972 giving
workers even more rights of codetermination about the workplace.

It is important to note that labor influence is said to be more legalis-
tic, or formalized into law, in Germany compared to other industrial nations, even though other countries in Europe are noted for strong labor
unions such as Sweden and Austria. Compared to several other European nations, Germany, in fact, has a lower rate of unionization (the percentage of workers belonging to unions), but this is misleading. It can be
said that despite the lower rate of unionization in Germany, workers
have more influence because: (1) the ties between works councils and
unions are more important than the number of workers who actually

join a union in the company; and (2) workers rights are more fixed in law and not as dependent upon what kind of government happens to be in office at the time. With this situation, a division of labor has developed especially between union leaders and works councils: Unions work for wage and other agreements affecting German workers generally—often through political action and threats of strike—while works councils see that these wider agreements and already existing labor rights are upheld on each individual shop floor, at times preventing organizational innovations.

A few examples of the rights afforded workers under the codetermination law will be useful for American readers who will find the situation surprising compared to their own country. Under the expanded 1972 laws, workers must be given extensive information about all matters affecting them and the whole company. Works councils must be consulted on any changes in policies concerning work time arrangements, overtime, work breaks, vacation times, plant wage systems, the introduction of new technologies, and any other alterations in the work environment, as well as the hiring, transfer, reclassification, or firing of workers. Thus, corporate managers "must secure (in advance) the consent of the works council on a range of personnel decisions affecting individual workers, including job assignments, classifications and reclassification, and transfers [paragraph 99 of the Works Constitutions Act]" (Thelen 1991:101). After consulting with the works council on issues, it is sometimes possible for managers to go against a works council vote, but to do so is usually very time consuming because of the extensive rights for challenge given to workers in a labor court system.[9]

Returning for a moment to Weber's multidimensional view of social stratification, it should be evident that what distinguishes American workers from German workers is that German workers have gained power through the political system and this power translates into the legal authority structure of German corporations. Following only a one-dimensional view of social stratification, or Marx's focus on economic ownership alone, we would have no clue why German workers have so much pay, benefits, and protection compared to their American brothers and sisters in the workplace.

GENDER INEQUALITIES

We now address a characteristic of German social stratification that is in some ways opposite of what we have just seen: While income inequality in general is quite low in Germany, and while German workers have some of the highest salaries in the world, German women do not fare as well. Germany has one of the highest levels of gender inequality among advanced industrial societies. We first consider some data comparing gender inequalities.

With respect to the male/female income ratio across all types of jobs, neither Germany nor the United States do very well: In Germany, females on average make about 73 percent of the average male income, while the figure in the United States is 74 percent (Kerbo 1996:293). Several industrial nations have male/female income ratios that are much higher. And when we start combining many other aspects of gender equality/inequality, the picture for Germany does not improve.

One of the most interesting indicators comes from the United Nations' Human Development Index (HDI). This index is a composite of income, wealth, employment, education, and health indicators, along with other indicators measuring the overall standard of living. For the first time in 1993, the United Nations published a separate Human Development Index for women in 33 countries. The level of gender inequality within each nation is then estimated by subtracting the gender index for each country from its overall Human Development Index. The "gender gap" in Human Development scores is shown in Table 5–2. Among the nations included, the lowest gender gap is found in Sweden, while the highest score is found in South Korea. It is important to keep in mind that the standard of living, level of income, education, and so forth are all far higher in South Korea than in the next higher country, Kenya, as well as most others. The point of reference is the gap between males and females in each country, not comparative standards of living for females in each country. For example, while Japan had the highest HDI score overall, it jumps to 17th with respect to the gender gap. Sweden, on the other hand, is fifth on the overall HDI but moves to first place with its low gender gap. Germany is another country with a relatively high overall HDI rank that falls significantly with its gender gap ranking.

Examination of the data in Table 5–2 indicates that the German-speaking countries of Switzerland, Austria, and Germany all have comparatively high levels of gender inequality, which suggests that culture (their ways of life) is involved. Historians agree that the old Germanic culture contains what most Americans would call *sexism*, or at best *traditional gender role separation* (see Craig 1991:147–61). Opinion poll data from Germany continue to indicate the presence of what would be called *more traditional gender roles* and *gender role separation*. For example, in 1985, 92 percent of German men living with a woman claimed never to have done any housework (Glatzer et al. 1992:105). Similarly, in 1985, 57 percent of women and 59 percent of men agreed that a woman can have either a career or be a mother, but not both. As for another indicator of traditional gender role separation, there continues to be no women allowed in the German military.

German government policy and legislation follow this pattern of role separation. It was only in 1957 that German law was changed so that the father no longer had "sole power of representation and decision in the case of differences of opinion between parents" (Glatzer et al. 1992:103). Also,

TABLE 5-2

The Human Development Index Gender Gap
for 33 Nations, 1993

Rank	Country	HDI Gender Gap	Rank	Country	HDI Gender Gap
1	Sweden	−5.7%	18	Portugal	−21.2%
2	Norway	−9.9	19	Switzerland	−21.5
3	Denmark	−9.9	20	Ireland	−22.2
4	Finland	−10.0	21	Japan	−22.4
5	New Zealand	−10.9	22	Greece	−23.4
6	France	−11.0	23	Myanmar	−23.8
7	Australia	−12.3	24	Luxembourg	−24.4
8	Paraguay	−14.8	25	Sri Lanka	−24.7
9	Netherlands	−14.8	26	Swaziland	−24.9
10	Britain	−15.1	27	Philippines	−25.2
11	Belgium	−15.1	28	Costa Rica	−25.8
12	Czechoslovakia	−15.5	29	Cyprus	−26.3
13	U.S.A.	−15.6	30	Singapore	−31.1
14	Canada	−16.9	31	Hong Kong	−32.3
15	Italy	−17.3	32	Kenya	−34.7
16	Austria	−17.9	33	South Korea	−36.4
17	Germany	−19.7			

Source: United Nations, Human Development Report, 1993.

we have seen that German labor laws are rather strict in supporting high minimum wages compared to the United States. There are, however, legal exceptions, such as in the "light wages groups" (Leichtlohngruppen): occupations or jobs that can be given lower wages. As you might expect most of these jobs are held by women (Glatzer et al. 1992:106).

Considering the actual occupational attainment of women, we find German women ranked even lower than women in other European countries and North America (Holtmann and Strasser 1990:12–13). Looked at another way, there is an even greater "glass ceiling" effect in Germany because women are less likely to be promoted into positions of authority (Hannan, Schomann, and Blossfeld 1990). For example, while over 40 percent of university students were women in 1995, and over one-third of PhDs went to women, only 8.5 percent of the top civil servants and judges were women, and only about 1 out of 20 (i.e., 5.7 percent) university professors were women (Parkes 1997:110).

Throughout the world there is also the problem of "gender labeling" of jobs: Jobs labeled as female tend to have lower pay even for the same education and skill levels as higher paying jobs labeled male. In Germany, the concentration of women in these "female jobs" is high and has remained high. In 1925, for example, 82 percent of all women employed in Germany were found in only 10 "female occupations." By 1982, 70 percent of German women were still employed in the same 10 female occupations (Glatzer et al. 1992:106). In a great contrast to the United States, few German women are found in male occupations such as engineering, and women in Germany are especially underrepresented in university and CEO positions.

Another important reason women have lower occupational attainment is that women in Germany receive less education than women in other industrial nations (Koenig 1987:76). This is especially the case in the very important apprenticeship training which is tied to obtaining highly skilled and highly paid jobs (Glatzer et al. 1992:105). But in addition to this, there is less "payoff" for German women compared to women in other countries when women do receive more education (Hannan, Schomann, and Blossfeld 1990). Finally, consistent with research from other countries, German women are more often than men employed in smaller companies that have lower pay for all workers, men and women (Carroll and Mayer 1986; Hannan, Schomann, and Blossfeld 1990).

In recent years there has been a relatively strong women's movement in Germany, along with increasing discontent among German women with respect to their position in the society (Hoffmeister and Tubach 1992:183–190). Research also indicates that there is a bigger difference in the attitudes toward women's rights and gender inequalities among younger versus older women in Germany than in other industrial nations (Davis and Robinson 1991). Some of the growing discontent among younger German women is reflected in other figures. For example, divorce in Germany is on the rise, and 70 percent of divorces are initiated by women rather than men. In addition, over 35 percent of German households are now led by singles, with about 30 percent of women between 18 and 65 unmarried (Hoffmeister and Tubach 1992:187). This situation is a likely reason why, when Germans are asked about the ideal family, only 25 percent now agree that the ideal is a two-parent family, compared to over 50 percent for the United States (*New York Times*, March 27, 1996).

It would seem, therefore, that Germany is in a critical period of gender conflict. Coming years could bring significant change, also expedited by the new Social Democrat–Green government coalition. Germany may experience change more like the one now occurring in the United States with slowly reduced gender inequalities (Kerbo 1996:Chapter 10). Much still depends on other critical changes in the German economy and European unification, which are considered in more detail later in this book.

SOCIAL MOBILITY AND STATUS ATTAINMENT

One of the most important questions about social stratification in a society relates to equality of opportunity: What are someone's chances of moving up or down the stratification system, and why? These questions address the subject of **social mobility,** which considers the amount of such movement in a society, and **status attainment,** which considers more directly what causes some people to move up from where their parents were on the social ladder.

We can be rather brief on this subject, however, because despite some small differences, we generally find broad similarities between Germany, the United States, and most other advanced industrial societies. We are also saying that the United States is no more the "land of opportunity" than most other industrial societies, including Germany. (The exceptions are racial and ethnic minorities, as we will see in the chapter on social problems.) Becoming a modern industrial society, in fact, has a considerable influence on the nature of social stratification in a country. This is especially true with respect to the extent to which social mobility is due to the creation of new jobs or to a change of values, that is, for example, how easy or difficult it is to enter the ranks of the elite (Ishida, Goldthorpe, and Erikson 1991; Erikson and Goldthorpe 1992).

Before World War II, and much earlier, there is some evidence for low social mobility in Germany (Spohn and Bodemann 1989). But today, for example, research by Kappelhoff and Teckenberg (1987) compared German data on this subject with the large and now famous American data set by Featherman and Hauser (1978). Most generally, the German researchers concluded that rates of social mobility in the two countries are broadly comparable. This is particularly so for the intergenerational mobility rate for a person's first job (compared to that of his or her parents). Over a person's lifetime career, however, there is somewhat more social mobility in the United States compared to Germany. One simple reason for this difference is that Germans change jobs less often than do people in the United States. In this respect, Germans are more similar to Japanese than to Americans.

A more complex reason for less career mobility in Germany compared to the United States involves important differences in educational systems (Kappelhoff and Teckenberg 1987; Blossfeld 1987:112). As we describe in the next chapter, Germany's educational system focuses more on jobs. Thus, with more job-specific training in the early years of a person's life, there are fewer chances or reasons to change to a different type of job, nor is this expected.

There is one more point to be made about social mobility in Germany: Kappelhoff and Teckenberg (1987:46) note that Germans seem to take a more collective attitude toward improving their life chances and that of their fellow workers, in contrast to the more individualistic solutions for Americans. In other words, Germans are more likely to stay put in a job and work to increase the pay and improve working conditions for themselves and fellow workers. Americans, on the other hand, see flight from a particular job as the main method of improving their standard of living and life chances. The differences in attitude may seem subtle, but they have profound implications for the nature of class conflicts and class power in Germany compared to the United States. This attitudinal difference has obvious implications for the power of unions and collective worker action in Germany and is no doubt related to a greater focus on unions and work laws, as we have already seen.

THE GERMAN UPPER CLASS

We have seen that Germany has less income inequality than the United States, and certainly more working class power and influence. However, this does not mean that a German upper class no longer exists. There remains something of an **upper class** of wealthy families who have extensive political as well as economic power in Germany. However, as you would expect with what we have described in this chapter and the previous one, this upper class is smaller and less powerful than it used to be.

As defeated world powers that developed late compared to other industrial societies, and were largely destroyed after World War II, Japan and Germany invite many comparisons. With respect to a wealthy upper class, there are a number of similarities—both before and after World War II. There also have been many differences. One similarity is that some very wealthy families emerged at about the time of rapid industrialization in the second half of the 1800s, though Germany never had as great a concentration of wealth in the pre-war period as did Japan.

Also among the similarities, parts of the upper class lost much of their wealth after World War II. Here, however, the comparison of Germany to Japan must certainly be seen as a matter of degree: We observe much more continuity of wealth in pre– and post–World War II Germany than in Japan, and very few of the big German corporations were broken up as were the largest *zaibatsu* in Japan (Broom and Shay 1992; Spohn and Bodemann 1989:85–87).[10] In Japan, over 90 percent of the wealth of the richest families was taken away soon after the war (Kerbo and McKinstry 1995:51–52). All of this means that upper class and corporate class power remains in Germany, somewhat more like in the present-day United States. Again, however, there are some differences that must be addressed if we are to understand the position and power of the current upper class in Germany.

As noted earlier, as of 1991 Germany ranked third in the world with respect to billionaires (*Forbes*, July 23, 1990; July 22, 1991, October 21, 1991; Shapiro 1992:74). In overall numbers, the United States has more than twice as many billionaires as Japan and Germany despite war devastation; however, Japan and Germany do have their share. Interestingly, Germany actually has a slightly higher concentration of billionaires per population than the United States or Japan, though with respect to this statistic Germany is third behind Hong Kong and Switzerland. Equally important to note is that unlike Japan, where most billionaires today are postwar in origin and generally not the most powerful people in the economy (Kerbo and McKinstry 1995:Chapter 4), German billionaires have much more continuity and more corporate power.

One of the most useful studies of current German billionaires was conducted by Broom and Shay (1992). Of the 43 billionaires in this data set from Germany, well over half of the family fortunes date back before World War II, and sometimes much further back. Six of the billionaire families originated before the 19th century. For example, "the youngest billionaire on the Forbes and Fortune rosters, eight-year-old Prince Albert von Thurn und Taxis, is twelfth in a family line that founded the Holy Roman Empire's postal service" (Broom and Shay 1992:4).

Another of the richest families in Germany today, the Haniels of the Ruhr industrial area of Germany, "date back 235 years to an ancestor to whom Frederick the Great granted the right to build a Duisburg warehouse" (Broom and Shay 1992:5). Today, Haniel family members hold about $5.3 billion in assets.

We should not miss the Krupp family wealth, so important to Germany in arms production during many wars. The last Krupp family member died in 1986, though he had dropped the Krupp family name by 1966 and renounced his inheritance because of Krupp corporate support of Hitler and the building of concentration camps during World War II (though he did agree to keep an annual allowance of $900,000 paid by the Krupp Foundation). The Krupp wealth dates back to the Thirty Years War (1618–48) when they made gun barrels for the Prussian Army.

As for a more recent billionaire family, the Bosch family fortune was established by Robert Bosch, who began making such things as electrical devices in 1886.

The real takeoff for these pre–World War II family fortunes goes back primarily to Germany's industrial expansion in the second half of the 1800s, even for most of the families who had wealth before this time. Three of the most wealthy after World War II (Krupp, Thyssen, and Haniel), for example, made much of their wealth during the second half of the 1800s in the Ruhr industrial area around Duisburg, Essen, and Bochum. Great wealth was also emerging from the growth of big German banks at that time. The biggest of them today, the Deutsche Bank, was established by the Siemens, a famous upper class family of today (Broom and Shay 1992: 5–6).

Elite Unity

As many studies of the upper class in the United States and other countries suggest, a unified upper class or elite is far more powerful economically and politically than a divided elite (Domhoff 1983, 1998). Compared to Japan's elite, the German elite is less unified and less interconnected. But then, no group of elites in a modern industrial society is even close to the unity, organization, and overlap found in Japan. Also, in Germany there is very little of what is called *amakudari* in Japan—moving from powerful government ministry positions into top corporate positions later in life. The German bureaucratic elite is much more likely to remain in their government positions until they retire—and really retire rather than moving to a corporate position or into politics as in Japan. There are a fair number of former bureaucrats in the German parliament (Bundestag), but almost all of these were only lower level bureaucrats before they became politicians (Dietrich 1991:280–82).

German corporate elites do not move in the other direction either, that is, enter top government bureaucratic positions as they do in the United States (over 2,000 of them every time a new president takes office). Thus, in contrast to the United States, "Entry into each service level normally occurs only at the lowest rung of the career ladder. Promotion, heavily influenced by seniority, moves the bureaucrat upward through his or her service level. Lateral entry into intermediate career ranks, or promotion from one service level to another, is rare" (Dietrich 1991:280).

To the extent that there is some upper class or elite unity in Germany, however, it arises primarily from common socialization experiences at a few of the top German universities. As Dahrendorf (1979:225) writes, "The law faculties of German universities accomplish for German society what the exclusive Public Schools do for the English, and the *grandes écoles* for the French. In them the elite receives its training." But it is not just the formal coursework that is most important. "Student activities and political groups, along with a heavy social schedule, are an important part of university life. In the law faculties of German universities [more like business colleges in the United States], a future elite is not only educated but socialized" (Dietrich 1991:280). The recent Potsdam elite study, which includes for the first time East German data, also confirms the continuing relevance of descent independent of education, though to a less degree. While opportunities to move into elite positions have generally improved over the years, women are still disadvantaged, though also to a less extent (Buerklin et al. 1997). Having said this, however, we must note the claims that today in Germany elite education and corresponding social activities forming elite networks are less widespread than they were 10 or 20 years ago due to the continued rejection of elitism in German society (Thies 1996:286).

Because elite unity is less in Germany than in Japan, however, it does not follow that the state and corporate sectors are in constant opposition. Rather, there is organization and cooperation—state guidance and economic planning with corporate and state alliance—to a much greater degree than in the United States. Habermas (1984) refers to the system as "liberal-corporatist capitalism," while others just use the term *corporatist* system (Dietrich 1991:277).

There is another level to the cooperation and mutual planning in postwar German society that is even more of a contrast to the system of power and social stratification in the United States. As mentioned above, because of German labor laws, the stock a person or bank holds in a particular corporation does not necessarily bring as much power in Germany as it does again in the United States. Workers in German corporations hold half of the board of director positions, though without the correspondent income and prestige. They are representative of the employee's side usually without owning any shares of the corporation. Thus, it is somewhat ironic that, while there may be an older upper class in Germany with more of their corporate stock in the original family corporations, this upper class has less power over these corporations than wealthy stockholders in American corporations. Again, as we have noted throughout this chapter, without understanding the dimensions of social stratification, and in this case the legal authority of the working class in postwar Germany, one cannot accurately judge the influence of what might otherwise seem to be a much more powerful and rich German upper class. In this sense it might well be that what was said in the 1920s was correct: Because the big industrialists, who constitute an important part of the upper class, could never achieve the riches of a true ruling class as aristocrats had before, they turned to Hitler. Before the war the aristocrats had prevented them from becoming the ruling clan, while after World War I the Social Democrats and the labor movement had a turn.

CONCLUSION

On the subject of social stratification in Germany, the most striking aspect, when compared to most other industrial nations and particularly the United States, is the low-level income inequality and the significant working class influence or power. Also, however, when compared to the United States especially, an important difference is the continued importance of status ranking in Germany. To understand these differences it is important to recognize the multidimensional view of social stratification from Max Weber. We have shown why income inequality has been reduced in Germany. This is largely due to the power obtained by the German working class and middle class through work laws and the power of unions.

CHAPTER 6

The Family

In this chapter and the following we describe some of the most important institutions in modern societies—the family, religion, and education. This chapter begins with the most basic institution throughout the history of human societies, the family.

The family, in fact, is often referred to by sociologists as the *master institution* because of its central importance, and because the family or clan organization served the social functions of all institutions in the earliest human societies about 10,000 years ago (Lenski, Lenski, and Nolan 1991). As societies evolved from hunting and gathering to modern industrial societies, other institutions developed, such as religion, the political system, the economy, and education, to slowly take over some of the tasks once performed by the family.

As agricultural societies evolved into advanced industrial societies around the world, once again, the family changed as well. As in other European countries and the United States, the **nuclear family,** consisting of at least a husband and a wife or a single parent with one child, has become the dominant form of family structure in Germany since the middle of the 20th century. However, as we will see in more detail, even the nuclear family in Germany has recently lost its monopoly as the basic system of procreation and socialization as more people decide to stay single or live "apart together" (that is, consider themselves a couple but maintain separate living arrangements). The German divorce rate also has gone up steadily in recent decades, especially since a new divorce law went into effect in 1977 making divorce easier. In addition, the number of women deciding to have children without getting married, as we will see, has increased rather dramatically in Germany. Thus, the concept of "life phase partnership" has emerged wherein a couple chooses to live together in a relationship—married or unmarried—considered by both to be only temporary, while "non-marital partnerships" are not really alternatives to marriage but rather trial marriages leading to a new "standard life phase" (Schäfers 1995:296–98).

Before we consider the German family today in more detail, however, it is useful to gain a historical perspective on the German family. A historical perspective allows us to understand to what extent the family has changed, and some of the reasons for and consequences of the changes.

THE FAMILY SYSTEM BEFORE WORLD WAR II

During the last two centuries, as the society at large evolved so did Germany's family structure. In preindustrial society German families were primarily **extended families** in contrast to **nuclear,** and even more **patriarchical** (male dominated) than in most other European societies. As was common all over the world in preindustrial societies, the place where the family lived was also the center of work and production. Occupational and private spheres were yet to be extensively separated. This is to say that the farm, the blacksmith shop, or the small merchant did not have a separate place of work from the family, and in fact family members usually contributed not only to the economic tasks at hand but also to education and care of the aged.

In preindustrial times, *family* referred not only to blood relatives: Apprentices or journeymen as well as farm laborers belonged to the family and lived under one roof with the patriarchic head of the household, his wife, his children, and often his or his wife's parents. Such three-generation families, which is to say, **extended families,** could be found in aristocratic households as well as on farms or in workshops. Apprentices could not afford to marry, while journeymen and farm workers were not allowed to marry.

With the rise of capitalism and the development of industrialization, as well as the emergence of a new middle class in the 19th century, a new family system developed that differed from that of the extended family. With the separation of work and family life, privacy became possible, and more extensive emotional ties could grow among family members. The division of labor in the workplace spread to the home with the husband as the only breadwinner, while his wife brought up the children, did the housework, and cared for the welfare of the family (Strasser and Haack 1985:94).

With Germany's industrialization in the second half of the 19th century and the expansion of its economic potential until 1914, millions of people migrated mostly from the poor rural areas in the east to the industrial regions in the west. Industrial workers and their families often lived in company housing near the factories. In the countryside, the multigeneration family survived to some extent, though not unaffected by changes due to the world wars, the Great Depression in the 1930s, and the "economic miracle" in the 1960s.

Most urban industrial workers lived in poverty due to the glut of unskilled and semiskilled manual workers in the labor market. As a result of low wages, very often women and children also had to work in order for the family to obtain basic necessities. In the Ruhr industrial area it was quite normal for these families to share their only sleeping room with homeless workers or unemployed people. These people, called *Schlafburschen*, paid rent, sometimes an important additional income for the family. These circumstances, in turn, led to less privacy and stressful living conditions among working class family members (Geissler 1996:37).

Theodor Geiger (1891–1952), an astute observer of German society, interpreted the change in family structure as a differentiation of social life. Accordingly, modern life is characterized by a dualism of the aloof public sphere and the intimate private sphere—what other sociologists have described as the functional differentiation characteristic of all modern societies (Geiger 1932; Strasser and Randall 1981:158). In addition, during the first half of the 20th century, two world wars cut millions of family ties and changed considerably the structure of the German population: Millions of wives lost their husbands and thousands of young people grew up as orphans.

POSTWAR DEVELOPMENTS

Emerging from the middle-class family system of the industrialization period, the nuclear family has been the dominant system in both the East and the West German states. Growing prosperity in the postwar decades made the 1960s Germany's "golden age of marriages" (Pross 1971). During that decade, 95 percent of all West Germans had been married one or more times, and 94 percent of all children were born "legitimately" (Kaufmann 1975). In East Germany, the marriage rate was about the same as in the West (Kaufmann 1975; Dorbritz and Gärtner 1995). Both parts of Germany regarded family and marriage as basic institutions to be protected by law. Nevertheless, they differed with respect to women's equality and its consequences for family life.

In the former GDR, the role expectations of women especially differed from those in West Germany. Women were expected to fulfill three social functions: housewives, wage earners, and active political participants. The GDR constitution emphasized this ideal of a child-loving, working, and participating woman. Both parents were obliged by law to take care of the household and to rear their children. Hence, special institutions were set up to support women's interests in every factory, government agency, school, or university. In addition, a variety of programs were designed to help working or studying women. For example, and in sharp contrast to West Germany, day care centers existed for all children and each university provided a nursery school for students with children. Finally, working or studying mothers profited from financial aid programs and extra holidays.

Undoubtedly, the communist regime did a great deal for the realization of women's rights. However, at the same time as "emancipation by law" led to better opportunities for women in occupational and social life, it also reinforced, in some respect at least, women's traditional roles as housewives and mothers. For example, due to decreasing birth rates in the 1960s and 1970s, the communist regime appealed to its female citizens to have more babies. "Socialist families" were eventually expected to bring up at least two children. Thus, the communist regime did a lot to promote the image of a politically active working mother, while at the same time actually holding her responsible for all the housework in her spare time (Geissler 1996:295; Erbsloeh et al. 1990:151).

In West Germany the idea of women being active in the public sphere of work and politics was at first rejected. However, the West German model of a "housewife marriage" has become less acceptable in the wake of the family reform law of 1977. Even today there are not enough part-time nursery schools for children and day care facilities for only 4 percent of all school children under the age of 10 (Geissler 1996:294). Hence, opportunities for women with children to pursue a career are restricted.

MODERNITY, AFFLUENCE, AND THEIR IMPACT ON THE FAMILY

Growing prosperity, more opportunities for men and women to attend schools and universities, and increased social and geographical mobility have contributed to the greater independence of individuals and a pluralization of lifestyles in German society. Traditional values stressing family duties, economic success, and social security have been more and more superseded by concerns for individual self-realization, quality of life, and what many would call hedonism (Schulze-Buschoff 1995:7; Inglehart 1989).

Since the 1960s, more women tend to start a career first and marry later. Moreover, the West German educational reforms of the 1970s led to a higher percentage of female, rural, and working class students. At the same time, the contraceptive pill evoked both sexual liberation and, in the long run, greater equality of opportunity.

As in many European countries, the third decade of life has become a postadolescent period in many individuals' lives (Schäfers 1995:123). However, unlike American students, German students need more years of study and usually enter the labor market much later. Again, we see changes that led to more independence and options in the lifestyles of German men and women.

New Ways of Living Together

In the last quarter of the 20th century, more Germans have tended to remain single or to choose alternative ways of living together. In 1995, for example, 25 percent of all singles between 18 and 55 years of age were in a partnership and yet lived "apart together," maintaining separate households while still considering themselves a couple (Meyer 1996:325). Social and geographical mobility also led to an increasing number of so-called commuter marriages: couples who share an apartment but do not marry until the birth of their first child. As confirmed by a recent study on nonmarital couples and their children, most of these "wild marriages" are "legalized" once the first child is on the way or born. In 1995, 1.5 percent of all German households were listed as nonmarital companionships with children (Bertram 1997). In addition, the number of singles sharing an apartment has increased, as has the number of single parents. Singles sharing an apartment are predominantly young and well educated. However, unmarried couples who live together can be found among all social classes and age groups (Schäfers 1995:298).

New ways of living together or apart have gradually been accepted in German society. In the 1960s, for example, bringing up a child without being married was socially not acceptable. Although nowadays most couples still marry before the first child is born, there is no longer any strongly felt obligation to do so, but wild marriages are by far not as common as official marriages. In earlier decades, however, single mothers were often stigmatized, and in some cases even forced to give up their newborns for adoption. Further, a young unmarried couple had great difficulties in finding an apartment or even a hotel room to spend holidays together. Today it is quite common for single mothers or even fathers to bring up their children alone.

THE DEMOGRAPHY OF THE GERMAN FAMILY

In 1994, 77.1 percent of all Germans between 30 and 65 were married and lived together with their partners. In 1970, 90 percent of all West German men and 97 percent of all West German women were married. But in striking contrast, by 1994 only 53 percent of all men and 60 percent of all women married at least once in their lifetime (Dorbritz and Gärtner 1995). In other words, some 40 percent of the Germans who belong to the generation after the 60s' "golden age of marriage" are not married. Individuals between 20 and 30 years of age usually have several relationships before they get married. As a consequence, the average age at first marriage has gone up. In 1960, women married on average at age 23, but by 1994 the average age at first marriage was almost 27. Men were 26 years old at the time of first marriage in 1960 but were over 29 years old by 1994. A result of this is that now women are older when their first baby is born: The average age was 24.3 years in 1970 but 27.3 years by 1993 (Dorbritz and Gärtner 1995).

In contrast to a common assumption, a prolonged postadolescent period and more time spent in partnerships before marriage do not always lead to a stable family. Like many other industrial nations, Germany has a high divorce rate. About 30 percent of all married couples eventually get divorced, while in cities alone almost every second marriage will end in divorce (Statistisches Bundesamt 1995:34). The number of divorces has quadrupled since the 1950s (Schulze-Buschoff 1995:6). Most divorced couples split up between their third and the sixth year of marriage. This does not mean though that the institution of marriage or the nuclear family system is outdated. About 30 percent of divorcees remarry and 80 percent of Germans continue to say that they prefer to live in a family and have children.

Due to the rising frequency of divorces, the number of children living with only one parent has increased. In 1992, approximately half of all divorced couples had children. The number of these "orphans by divorce" (as they are referred to in Germany) more than doubled between 1960 and 1993 (Meyer 1996:314).

Another consequence of the above changes is a dramatic slowdown in the **fertility rate** in Germany. In the United States today, the total fertility rate (children born per reproductive woman) is about 2.1 compared to about 1.4 in Germany. Considering that about 2.1 children per woman are necessary to keep a country's population stable, in the absence of immigration into Germany, in a couple of centuries there will be no Germans left (Europäische Kommission 1996:15). Germany is now experiencing its lowest fertility rate in history (*International Herald Tribune*, July 11, 1998). Because of this another milestone will be passed before the 21st century begins: There will be more Germans over 60 years of age than under 20 years of age.

There are several reasons for the decrease in Germany's fertility rate. For example, the number of singles and single-parent families has increased. In 1992, 14.1 percent of all West German families with children under 18 were single-parent families, as compared to 9 percent in 1976. The number of male single parents has also gone up: 17 percent of all single parents were men in 1993 (Meyer 1996:322). Also, there are an increasing number of families who choose to have only one child. Of course, modern contraceptives, which allow for greater freedom in family planning, have been a major factor in lower fertility. Many women plan their pregnancies so that their careers are not interrupted at an unsuitable point. Another phenomenon is more widespread in Germany than in the United States: DINKS—double income, no kids. At the end of the 1980s, 21 percent of all West German women between 35 and 39 years were childless. By the mid-1990s, the rate had risen to 24 percent (Schwarz 1995).

These developments, of course, also reflect changing attitudes toward having children. It is estimated that one-third of all German women today do not want children (Meyer 1996:321). In 1987, 77 percent of all West Germans believed that people without children had a better life than families or single parents (Meyer 1996:322). Children compete not only with the values of personal freedom and self-realization but also with opportunities for leisure activities such as sports, traveling, and continuing education. Having children may then be regarded as a burden and in conflict with a modern lifestyle, especially with the positive side of the "fun society" (Sustek 1995:21; Schulze 1995).

We should note in closing this section, however, that the pluralization of the family structure and the changes described above are not found equally in all social classes in Germany. Single parents, unmarried couples, and couples "living apart together" predominantly belong to the well-educated and prosperous groups of society. While the divorce rate in cities is much higher than in rural areas, people with well-to-do backgrounds are more affected by divorce, in part, perhaps, because they can afford it (Burkart 1995:9).

Different Developments in East and West Germany

Before German reunification, a pluralization of lifestyles had already taken place in both parts of the country. Although the East German regime always insisted on the nuclear family system with many children, East Germany actually had higher rates of divorce and single-parent households than did West Germany. There were also more unmarried women in East Germany before the Berlin Wall came down, and there were fewer singles than in West Germany today. During the 1980s, a nuclear family with both parents working was the most common living arrangement for young adults in the GDR. In West Germany, however, most young adults were singles (Drauschke and Stolzenberg 1995:276).

In the 1990s, the East German family shows new and, to some extent, contradictory tendencies. With the newly implemented West German laws pertaining to family arrangements and divorce, the number of divorces decreased from 2.0 to 0.6 per 1,000 marriages in East Germany within the first two years after reunification. However, in 1993, the divorce rate increased again, and the percentage of single-parent families rose from 14.7 in 1990 to 27.2 percent in 1995 (Hauser 1996:5). In addition, there is a strong tendency not to marry at all in East Germany. In 1990, 102,000 marriages were counted in East Germany (6.3 per 1,000 citizens), but by 1992 only 48,000 couples (3.1 per 1,000 citizens) married (Statistisches Bundesamt 1995:35). These tendencies may be regarded as a result of the transformation shock brought about by all the uncertainties East Germans were (and to some extent still are) exposed to after the GDR went out of existence in 1990 (Meyer 1996:316).

THE GERMAN FAMILY IN A COMPARATIVE CONTEXT

In contrast to the United States, all member states of the European Union (EU) have experienced major declines in the number of household members within the last 20 years. Similarly, and again in contrast to the

United States, there have been dramatic declines in the fertility rates of most EU members. In 1990, the average Western European household (including the Netherlands, Great Britain, Belgium, and France) had 2.6 persons. In the Mediterranean countries such as Italy, Greece, Portugal, and Spain, the average household size was 3.5 persons. With 2.3 persons, Germany and Denmark had the smallest household sizes (Hradil 1995:294).

In the Mediterranean countries and in Ireland, the fertility rates began to drop later than in Germany or Austria, but then the drop was even more dramatic, leaving those countries with the lowest fertility rates in the EU (between 1.1 and 1.4). As we already noted, with a fertility rate considerably below 2.1, most Western European countries are not able to keep their populations stable. Only the Scandinavian countries have experienced a rise in birth rates since the 1980s: Women in Denmark, Norway, and Sweden give birth to 1.7 to 2.1 babies on average (Europäische Kommission 1996:15). In 1997, the average fertility rate in the EU overall was 1.4 (Santel 1995:69).

In all EU countries, the average age at first marriage has risen within the last three decades. In 1990, people in Scandinavian countries married at the age of 26 to 28 years, with the average for Germans at 27 (Dorbritz and Gärtner 1995). At the same time, people in the Mediterranean countries married about two years earlier.

With respect to the stability of marriage, in most Western European countries, one-third or more of all married couples will get divorced later in life. In 1990, Scandinavian countries showed the highest divorce rates (43–44 divorces out of 100 marriages), while England was also high with 41 percent of marriages ending in divorce. Germany, therefore, has comparatively moderate rates of divorce (29 percent in the West and 22 percent in the East), though it is clearly a rising tendency. The Mediterranean countries (Spain, Italy, and Greece) and Ireland have the lowest divorce rates, mainly due to the influence of the Church (Catholic and Orthodox) which has made divorces illegal for decades (Hradil 1995:297).

In summary, compared to all European countries, Germany holds a middle position with respect to the range of change in the family structure. Compared to the United States, however, all of these European nations have experienced more change in the family structure with more divorces, fewer children, and more young people not getting married at all, or much later in life.

CONCLUSION

Within the past two centuries, Germany's family structure has changed considerably. In the course of industrialization, family size went down in practically all countries, in addition to other changes in the family. Industrialization has brought about many gender role changes: The husband emerged as the only breadwinner, and women became housewives in charge of the children's and other family members' care. The nuclear family advanced to the dominant form in the second half of the 20th century. In recent decades, greater independence for young people, the women's movement, economic prosperity, rising levels of education, increased mobility, and the pluralization of lifestyles have prompted changes toward a new order of gender roles in Germany and elsewhere in Europe.

Today, Germans are in a paradoxical situation. On the one hand, opinion polls show that four out of five Germans would like to live in a family and have children. In 1993, 76 percent considered the institution of family as being "very important"; for another 21 percent the family was at least "important" (Weick 1995). On the other hand, with the number of marriages decreasing, the divorce rate increasing, and the fertility rate decreasing as well, there are by far too few new births to keep the German population stable.

Because of all this, Germany faces another fundamental social, political, and economic challenge: The population is aging rapidly due to a low fertility rate and an increase in life expectancy. As a result, fewer people are in the labor force, which means there are fewer and fewer workers to pay into the pension system to take care of the elderly. How Germany and other European nations cope with these problems, and the changes they do or do not make, will be very instructive for Americans, who live in a society where many of these same changes are developing, though so far at a much slower rate.

CHAPTER 7

Religion and Education in Germany

In this final chapter on basic institutions in Germany we will first consider one of the oldest institutions in human societies, and then one of the newest. When human societies changed from hunting and gathering to agriculture, religion was one of the first institutions to develop as a separate institution from the clan system. As the sociological master Émile Durkheim noted in *The Elementary Forms of the Religious Life*, religion in all societies functions to promote social integration, unity of meanings, and moral values. Until the evolution of modern industrial societies, religious institutions also provided education, but education for social integration and moral values rather than for the professional and technical occupations needed to run a modern industrial society. With the evolution to modern industrial societies, then, a new institution emerged: educational systems to serve the new need of passing on technical information to the younger members of society.

It is worth noting that Germany, in fact, has contributed much to the world with respect to both of these institutions. For example, it was a German monk, Martin Luther, who started the social movement against the Catholic Church almost 500 years ago that established the Protestant Churches found all over the world today. And it was the Prussian government minister Wilhelm von Humboldt who in the early 1800s established a model for universities that stressed freedom of research and instruction. He also established the structure and content of secondary schools found around much of the world today (Raff 1988:47).

In this chapter we examine both of these institutions in Germany, outlining their basic characteristics, and comparing them to institutions in other advanced industrial nations, particularly the United States.

Funeral March in the Southern Countryside: Religious traditions remain strong in Germany, especially in the countryside, even though Germans generally score lower than Americans on the importance of religion in their lives. As in all societies, such traditions as the funeral march shown here help reconfirm community, church, and family as basic institutions in the society.

RELIGION IN GERMANY

Traveling through Germany today one could get the impression that Germans are quite religious. Beautiful churches are all over German cities and villages, and each city of any importance has at least one huge cathedral in its center. However, in contrast to the United States, such an impression is at least inaccurate, if not misleading. "To be honest, we have to admit that our present relationship with God is not an easy one," wrote the German sociologist F. X. Kaufmann (1989:196). Indeed polls attest to the growing indifference among Germans towards God and the Christian belief. As can be seen in Table 7–1, with the exception of the United States, religious indifference represents a trend noticeable throughout Western industrial societies. It seems people believe religion is no longer able to explain the world and provide a sense of meaning in their lives as was the case for centuries. Sociologists of religion even go as far as to say that religion must "niche-market" itself if it is to effectively compete against alternative organizations as a provider of emotion and meaning (for example, see Turner 1997).

TABLE 7-1

The Importance of Religion

Country	Who Believe in a God	Importance of Religion in Life (10-point scale)
United States	98%	8.55
Ireland	97	8.02
Spain	92	6.39
Italy	88	6.96
England	81	5.72
Germany (West)	80	5.67
France	65	4.72
Japan	62	4.49

Sources: *The Gallup Report,* May 1985, p. 52; Shapiro, World Values Survey (1992:40).

Still, Germany has a centuries-old tradition of religion and even today more than 52 million Germans belong to either the Protestant Church or Roman Catholic Church. As institutions of welfare and collective conscience, these churches are significant for the functioning of German society: They support the welfare state with a wide range of organizations and act to point out problematic developments in politics as well as in society as a whole.[11]

A chapter about religion in Germany can no longer cover only the Protestant and Roman Catholic Churches. Because of immigration, Islam has become the third largest religion in Germany. Thus, along with the main religions in Germany today, we will examine the place of Islam. In addition, we will describe the more critical view, and less tolerance, found in Germany toward what can be called *religious sects* when compared to the United States. First, however, we need to consider the place of religion in the history of Germany.

A History of Religion in Germany

In medieval Europe, church and state, religion and society, formed a unity, which contemporaries took for granted. The Roman Catholic Church represented the ultimate values accepted by the vast majority of people at the time. The shared religious beliefs and the daily routine of religious rituals helped maintain social order and supported the political system. Heretics were considered enemies by both the clerical and the secular powers.

The high point of papal and episcopal power in Europe is considered to be the period between the 11th and the 14th centuries. The pope ruled Rome much like a monarch and many of his bishops had become powerful sovereigns. Yet, the political and religious rule of the papal church was shaken in the early 16th century when the Protestant Reformation rang in a new era that led to radical changes in the social, political, and religious realms.

Martin Luther, a monk and professor of theology at Wittenberg University in Saxony, along with other pioneers of the Protestant Reformation, was determined to bring an end to the omnipotence of the Roman Catholic Church. In their view, the church had deteriorated into a secular and immoral power apparatus. For example, the Catholic Church would offer mitigation of penalties and release from purgatory (in other words, salvation) in return for cash. Religious glamour and the adoration of saints had become more important than Christian morals and the word of the Bible. The reformers wanted to establish a new Christian movement in its place, with no ceremonious pomp or devout rituals. They wanted the New Testament and the words and deeds of Christ to become once again the center of religious belief.

In many places the reformers were helped by secular sovereigns or political elites who had become ever more powerful and who opposed the power claims of the pope and the Catholic Church. These political elites thus supported the reform movement, which not only led to bloody wars over religion and power, but also to a division of the Christian religion. Two Christian churches came into existence in Europe: One was represented by Roman Catholicism, the papal church, and the other was Protestantism, which opposed Rome and sought radical reforms.

With the Protestant Reformation, the "disenchantment of the world," as described by Max Weber in *The Protestant Ethic and the Spirit of Capitalism,* and the decline of the churches took its course. Very gradually, religion lost its power of persuasion in terms of providing meaning to people's lives. But this reduction in religiosity also helped support the principles of Enlightenment in the 18th century: Science and rationality, personal autonomy and individual freedom became the magic words of the time. This meant a final loss of political power for the two churches because the system of religious norms and values was less able to discipline the membership and hold the community together. The nation and the *Vaterland* (fatherland), eventually the German nation state, became almost substitute religions (Muench 1996:44).

During the 19th century, religion and denomination ultimately moved from the public to the private sphere. The liberal, enlightened bourgeoisie (middle class and capitalists) chose the economy and the state. Being a Christian was increasingly reduced to acts of private and individual piety and the aspects of Christian teaching that had supported critical and even revolutionary ideals in the beginning vanished. The educated and the wealthy only cared about keeping up pious appearances, while the proletariat (working class) had initially not even been part of the Christian congregation. Individual piety, so characteristic of the bourgeoisie, was not something that the working people could make much use of (Kantzenbach 1975:426).

The decline of the churches, however, was not only due to a change in *mentality*. The churches were also affected by the fact that religious affairs were increasingly subjected to national supervision for the interests of the state. The situation escalated when the pope reaffirmed the legitimacy of his rule over all believers in 1870 through the Dogma of Infallibility. As a result, a "culture struggle," *Kulturkampf*, broke out in Germany as the Protestant chancellor of the German empire, Otto von Bismarck, struck against the rebellious Roman Catholic Church: The clergy was forbidden to utter political views and the interference of the state in church matters was extended. At the end of the culture struggle in 1887, the Catholic Church had failed to make the government accept its demands for more autonomy. The Protestant Church, elevated to the status of Prussian state church, was on Bismarck's side and supported his anti-Catholic Church policy.

It was only in the 20th century that the separation of church and state became reality in Germany. In 1919, after World War I and after the socialists and liberals (who were critical of the churches) had come to power, the new Weimar Constitution supported an ideologically neutral state with religious freedom as one of its principles. However, the constituent assembly was not yet ready for a radical separation of the church from the state as this would also have meant the end of clerical privileges. This is why the German churches hold a constitutionally special position in Germany even today.

The 1920s and 1930s, politically turbulent as they were, show how little power and self-confidence the churches had. Shaken by the revolutionary climate, the Protestants especially were lamenting the end of the *Kaiserreich*—the monarchy of God's Grace—and many of them eventually turned against the new democratic order of the Weimar Republic by supporting the German national movement, and later Hitler's National Socialism. The Catholic Church, too, was conservative and rejected the separation between church and state prescribed by the Weimar Constitution.

In the beginning of Hitler's Third Reich, the Nazis pretended to be pro-church. The religious traditions were rather deeply rooted and even ardent National Socialists were devoted churchgoers. Strictly speaking, Hitler and his party elites left no doubt that their only objective was the total enforcement of the National Socialist ideology. National Socialism, a kind of polit-religion, inevitably had to come into conflict with the churches.

At first, however, both the Protestant and Catholic Churches saw the Nazi regime in a positive light. The fight against Marxism and the support of the proud German nation, as well as the restoration of morality, order, and authority, made National Socialism inviting for Protestant and Catholic circles. The pro-authoritarian Catholic Church, which had vehemently fought against National Socialism before 1933, was enticed by Hitler with extensive legal guarantees (such as parochial schools, religious instruction, and autonomy over personnel) laid down in the *Reichs-*

konkordat with the Vatican of 1933. Hitler, therefore, succeeded in de-politicizing the clergy and gaining international legitimation.

Hitler's agreement with the pope, however, was merely a farce and soon the government waged a "war against the churches": Catholic and Protestant clergy were muzzled by the state and no longer allowed to express political views. Those who continued to do so, such as the now famous Martin Niemöller, were arrested and deported to concentration camps. Crucifixes were removed from classrooms, many parochial schools were closed down, and church organizations were prohibited. The churches could neither afford nor wanted to express open resistance; there was too much fear for one's own life and concern for one's institution.

In the end, however, the churches survived both National Socialism and World War II to become the most important moral authority of a traumatized and disoriented society in the postwar years. More than 90 percent of the population belonged to one of the two churches, which also played a significant role in rebuilding West Germany. In the meantime, in the Soviet-occupied eastern part of Germany, the former center of the Reformation, the new communist regime started abolishing the social roots of the churches. Even though the dechurching of the GDR proved more successful than the Nazis' struggle against the churches, Protestantism did not vanish. It skillfully oscillated between adjustment, a pro-regime attitude, and casual resistance.

The Churches and the State in the Federal Republic Today

The religious system of the Federal Republic of Germany today is dominated by the Protestant and Catholic Churches: 70 percent of Germans officially belong to either church (about 35 percent each), but the number of Christians who actively participate in services and parish life is much smaller. The proportion of Catholics who actually attend church services has gone down considerably, from almost 50 percent in 1960 to considerably less than 20 percent in the mid-1990s. For the Protestant church another trend holds true: Between 1975 and 1996, there was hardly any change, although only 5 percent of their members attend church (Statistisches Bundesamt 1996; EKD 1998a:18; EKD 1998b:3).

Nevertheless, the churches have considerable influence on the political, social, and cultural scenes. Not only are the German churches among the wealthiest in the world, their relationship with the political authorities and their participation in the educational process and the school system is not without significant effects.

As mentioned before, the privileges granted to the churches are rooted in the constitution dating back to the Weimar Republic during the 1920s. Thus, religious instruction in the Protestant and Catholic religions exists in most schools in Germany. Moreover, the churches are allowed to train their own teachers and theologians at state universities. As employers, the churches are not tied to public agreements on wages, rather they have their own "church law" on these issues. Churches are also independent in choosing the structures of internal organization they deem best. In doing so, they are not bound by any commitment to democratic principles.

The churches and the German state act at the same time as "social partners" in that both churches offer a number of public welfare services. The two major religious organizations within this charitable network are the *Caritas* and the *Diakonisches Werk*. They run hospitals, nursing homes, nursing care units, and mobile help services; they also take care of the distribution of food and clothing among the needy and provide lodging for the poor and the homeless. Furthermore, they support refugees and immigrants and are major contributors to Germany's development aid abroad.

As they play an important role in helping the state by operating a wide range of welfare programs, the churches receive financial assistance in return. That they can also rely on a lucrative church tax (collected for them by the government from employees' paychecks) amounting to 9 percent of the income tax of their members, helps explain why German churches fare so well (and are often so distant to their membership).

With their well-organized parishes, lay groups, nursery schools, recreational facilities, youth clubs, hospitals, and nursing homes, the churches dominate large parts of the social sector in the Federal Republic. Owing to their public presence, and based on numerous academies, faculties at state universities, institutions of adult education, religious instruction at schools, and their share in helping to preserve monuments, the churches are perhaps the most important single cultural institutions in Germany. They are also the country's largest employer. It goes without saying that they are backed by influential representatives and advocates in all areas of social life.

The Crisis of the Churches

In contrast to what is happening at the end of the 20th century in the United States, there is certainly no resurgence of Christianity in Germany. The conservative archbishop of Fulda, Johannes Dyba, has said, "We are in a state of free fall," when characterizing the relationship between the church and the German population (*Der Spiegel* 52, December 22, 1997:69). The fact that an increasing number of believers have turned away from the churches and the Christian doctrine, however, is neither new nor surprising: As the historical review has shown, the social influence of the churches has steadily decreased since the Reformation. Due to various "culture struggles" in the 19th and 20th centuries, their influence considerably diminished. The reunification process has obviously contributed to less religiosity in the Federal Republic of Germany as well. While in the old Federal Republic (before 1990) 84 percent of the population belonged to one of the churches, this number has now dropped to under 70 percent.[12]

For the dechurching of East Germany the socialist regime has been blamed. And yet the Protestant Church in the East became a major force of political resistance, without which the "peaceful revolution" by which East Germans abolished the communist government in 1989 would probably not have been possible. It is this kind of commitment that is responsible for the churches' higher recognition in East Germany as compared to their position in the more religious West Germany (Barz 1994).

As authorities that help provide people with meaning in life and society with moral cement, as described by Durkheim (1948) almost a century ago, the churches may seem obsolete in Germany today. Nowadays, these tasks are fulfilled by other institutions, such as the media, markets of lifestyle and popular culture, Greenpeace, the economy, science, politics, the legal system, and education. However, the Catholic Church, in particular, is partly responsible for its own misery. The rejection of extramarital sex, the contraceptive pill, and homosexual relationships, as well as the exclusion of women from the priesthood, are perceived as anachronistic by many Germans. Young Germans especially do not consider the church compatible with modern life.[13]

With the decline of the churches in Germany, however, many Germans believe there is a crisis of moral values and meaning in life. Collective orientations erode and moral ideas, it is believed, are no longer effectively internalized. In highly individualized societies, the individual is responsible for organizing his or her own life and deciding whether he or she is able and willing to live a religious life. The modern agencies of socialization such as the family, school, peers and the mass media, which contribute to the individual's development of a moral conscience as the churches used to, seem unable to provide religiously grounded values and norms. However, in contrast to the United States, there is no strong movement in Germany to revive church philosophy or make church membership more appealing to the population. It is unlikely that interest in the Christian churches will grow anytime soon, if at all, in Germany, while Americans become even more active in organized Christian religions.

Allah in Germany

Islam in Western Europe is often thought of as the religion of the "others," that is, the immigrants, be they guest workers or refugees (Abdullah 1993:21). With 2 to 3 million adherents, Islam is the third largest religious community in Germany following Protestantism and Catholicism.[14] The strong presence of Islam is primarily due to the Federal Republic's liberal immigration and refugee policy, which continued well into the 1990s. Most Muslims come from Turkey or are of Turkish descent. The majority of these Turkish immigrants were recruited as so-called guest-workers between 1960 and 1973, a time when economic growth was so rapid in Germany that there was a critical shortage of workers. However, as the Swiss novelist Max Frisch once remarked, "Workers had been called but people came."

Islam is a religion characterized by continuous devotion to God, unselfishness being one of its essential ideals. Excessive consumption, the use of alcohol and drugs, and sexual liberty are prohibited as they are considered to be harmful to both the individual and society. As a Western, consumption-oriented country, the Federal Republic has remained an alien and uncomfortable place for many Muslims to live (Meys and Sen 1986).

Even though Islam has come to represent the third largest religious community in Germany, its more than 2 million followers are a minority compared to Germany's 57 million Christians. In addition, Muslims are not held together by an organized, churchlike religion as is typical of Christians. Rather, Islam is divided into a variety of religious movements. In Germany, there are some 1,200 Islamic congregations representing all kinds of Muslims, among them fundamentalists, traditionalists, modernists, and heretics (Abdullah 1993:20).

Nevertheless, the times of "backyard mosques" or the hidden Islamic culture in German cities could soon be over. Practicing Muslims who have become more self-confident about their religious beliefs are trying to help their religion procure a stronger presence in the public sphere. Thus, in German cities the *Muezzin* is now heard more often calling his congregation to prayer (with the aid of a loudspeaker). This has led to a host of conflicts between resident Muslims, on the one hand, and the German population and the two main churches, on the other. So far, Protestant and Catholic churches have dominated the cities in terms of architecture with their large, widely visible church towers and the sound of church bells. Now they fear for their visible and audible exclusiveness. The debate over whether Islamic calls to prayer should be audible illustrates that many Germans reject the public presence of Islam, based on a deeply rooted fear of cultural alienation and religious intrusion.[15]

The situation for young Turks in Germany is changing quite rapidly, however. More often than not they are born in Germany and educated in German schools. They are much better trained than their parents and the proportion of Turkish students enrolled at German universities is continuously rising. The second generation of Turks in Germany benefits from their parents' social advancement as merchants, craftsmen, and shopkeepers who can afford a better education for their children. At the same time, these adolescents grow up in a social and cultural environment characterized by divergent world views and conflicting expectations.

On the one hand, they are expected to take advantage of educational and professional opportunities in Germany. On the other hand, their parents and relatives want them to keep up Islamic traditions as well. According to some studies, there is reason to believe that faced with this conflict, young Turks increasingly opt against Islam and the traditions of devoutness: 58 percent of them already distance themselves from Islam, and only 12 percent comply with their parents' religious traditions (Abdullah 1993:31).

Sects and the State

In Germany the term **sect** brings up a wide range of prejudices. Most people associate the term with religious delusion, fanaticism, and, above all, the practice of luring naive or unhappy young individuals into such religious groups. In recent years, the negative image of sects has increased as a result of the bloody, televised conflict between the US government and the American Davidian Sect in Waco, Texas, in 1993. Two years later, the Aum Sect was held responsible for a poison gas attack in the Tokyo subway. In Germany, the public debate centers around the Scientology organization, whose advertising campaign has drawn a great deal of international attention.

The *International Herald Tribune* (February 9,1997) published an "Open Letter to Helmut Kohl, Chancellor of the German Federal Republic," paid for by Scientology church members. The letter accused the German government of persecuting the followers of the Scientology church in much the same way as the Nazis persecuted the Jews ("In the 1930s, it was the Jews. Today it is the Scientologists."). The letter was signed by, among others, several famous Hollywood stars. Politicians of all major German political parties rigorously rejected the charges. Many Germans felt deeply insulted and agreed with Kohl's view that those who had signed this open letter knew nothing about contemporary Germany.

Scientology has indeed come under increasing political attack in Germany. For example, in two states, members of Scientology can no longer be employed in civil service jobs because these states question whether scientologists conform to democratic principles. The Christian Democratic Party bars scientologists from membership. And recently, the secretaries of the interior in these two German states have decided to have Scientology supervised by the Office for the Protection of the Constitution.

Based on the Federal Republic's concept of democracy, which allows active resistance to those whom it considers a threat, it is recognized as legitimate, at least in principle, for the state to investigate possibly dangerous and suspicious groups. Religious groups can claim no exemption—especially if they employ drastic and upsetting methods to interrogate members, who often have to pay large sums of money in order to attend special seminars offered by the organization (Valentin 1994).

With almost no chance of success, Scientology continues its struggle for recognition as a religious community in Germany. According to German courts, Scientology is not a church, but an internationally operating, sophisticated business enterprise. There is, of course, controversy over whether or not Scientology does pose a threat to the democratic order of the Federal Republic, especially since other European states (such as the

Netherlands, Austria, Spain, Great Britain, and Italy) are much more relaxed in dealing with Scientology, and the United States, by contrast, recognized the Scientology Church as a religious community in 1993.

CONCLUSION

Obviously, German society cannot be described as unreligious as long as the principles of Christianity are so deeply rooted in its constitution and laws, and in its people's customs, norms, and values. Also, one cannot ignore basic elements of Christian principles in the structure of the German welfare state.

However, despite the approaching end of the millennium, the times of spirituality in Germany seem to be over. Islam, too, which has entered Germany by way of migration, will probably not play a significant role in the foreseeable future.

The Protestant and Catholic Churches' wide-ranging social commitment, though, has made them invaluable to the functioning of German society. They are the centers of volunteer work, drawing people of all ages; they offer all kinds of leisure activities for the young; and they provide material assistance for those who are in need. Thus, they take care of those who are, at least to some extent, excluded from participating in the society, such as the homeless, old people, and asylum seekers. While severely affected by the current government budget cuts, as well as by an increase in the number of people who have left the church, as institutionalized religions they will continue to pervade much of the social fabric in Germany.

EDUCATION IN GERMANY

As industrial societies slowly emerged almost three centuries ago, as noted at the beginning of this chapter, the stage also was set for the emergence of a new institution. No longer could parents, close relatives, or religious leaders teach children all they would need to know for their future working lives. The institution of education had to develop if these new modernizing societies were to be possible (Lenski, Lenski, and Nolan 1991). Thus, when we look around the modern world today, we find great similarities in educational systems. Almost all societies require young people to attend schools until they are 14 to 18 years of age, and all of the modern societies have university systems to expand education for those who are to fill the more skilled professional and technical positions required in advanced industrial societies.

There are, however, many differences behind these similarities. For one thing, some nations do a better job in educating young people in the basics of math, science, and other subjects needed to run a modern society. We must admit that almost all other modern societies do a better job than American schools at the primary and secondary levels of education.

One of the most recent of the many international exam comparisons, the Third International Mathematics and Science Study *(Los Angeles Times,* Feb. 27, 1998), has again found American high school students substantially behind others in their knowledge. German students, as usual, scored above American students in every subject, and most often considerably above American students. The interesting conclusion of most of these studies is that while American elementary and middle school children compare well to young people of their own ages around the world, during the high school years American young people drop significantly.

With respect to colleges and universities, however, it can be said that those in the United States are among the best in the world. Despite von Humboldt's establishment of the model university philosophy about 200 years ago, the model was followed most closely in the United States. Of course, Hitler disrupted the best German universities during the 1930s and 1940s, and as a result of that many of the best physical and social scientists ended up at American universities. However, this brain drain, not only from Germany, continued for several decades after the war.

It is also important to recognize that more young people in the United States go on to colleges and universities than in other advanced industrial nations. Germany, on the other hand, follows an educational policy of more job-centered education on the high school level, and sending fewer young people on to universities for advanced education. For those who do enter universities in Germany, there is another difference: In a major contrast to the United States, university education in Germany is free. And, in fact, if your parents have an income at or below the average, you would also qualify for an additional stipend to help pay for other expenses while studying.

It is time to turn to more details of the German educational system: how it works, how it developed, and how it compares with the system of education in the United States.

The Educational System of the Federal Republic

As we have already seen, Germany is a federal state, which means that somewhat like the United States, each state, or *Land*, is responsible for the organization of its own school and university system. Most schools and universities are public (state owned and run), while the few private schools are run by the Protestant or Catholic Churches. As in the United States, the German educational system is divided into the primary, secondary and tertiary levels of education. Beyond this, though, the German educational system becomes much more complicated with a number of options for different kinds of education.

The traditional primary school *(Grundschule)* lasts for four years. A three-part school system, varying from state to state, constitutes secondary education: The *Hauptschule* provides fundamental education after elementary school, comprising grades 5 to 9 or 5 to 10 (i.e., with an optional 10th year). Today, the completion of the *Hauptschule* is considered the minimum education required by law. There is also the *Realschule,* which offers an intermediate degree at the end of the 10th grade that is considered more rigorous. The third option, the *Gymnasium* (comparable to a college prep high school), provides general education in nine years (grades 5 to 13) for those students expecting to enter a university. The last three years of the *Gymnasium* (grades 11 to 13) constitute the upper level of secondary education (*Sekundarstufe II*), at the end of which students graduate and are awarded the *Abitur,* which qualifies them for entrance to a university.

There is even more complexity and other educational options in the German system of education. For example, new vocationally specialized high schools (*Fachoberschulen*) provide a means of college entrance other than *Gymnasium,* while the *Gesamtschule* includes all levels of secondary education and leads to possible college entrance. These newer schools have been added as a means of promoting more equality of educational opportunity for students of less affluent families who did not have many opportunities to advance to the university level in the past.

The most important generalization about the German educational system is that there are college prep high schools and high schools primarily focused on vocational training, combining on-the-job training with an employer and education at some kind of vocational school. Training in each of the 370 skilled occupations in industry, commerce, agriculture, crafts, and the public sector normally lasts three years. Upon completion a graduate is awarded a certificate of apprenticeship or a similar certification recognizing the trainee as a competent practitioner of his or her occupation.

At the tertiary level, there are the traditional and technical universities, new reform universities, special colleges (*Fachhochschulen*) such as colleges of social work, and colleges of arts and music. In addition, there are *Gesamthochschulen,* which combine the principles of the more theoretically oriented universities and the more practically oriented *Fachhochschulen.* Due to the increasing numbers of students, access to many areas of study is restricted (currently, for example, in such fields as psychology, law, and medical studies). There are only a few private universities, mostly graduate schools of business administration, charging tuition and fees, as opposed to the free state university system (see Anweiler et al. 1992:530).

The Educational System of Communist East Germany until 1989

Soon after the end of World War II, the education systems in East and West Germany began drifting apart. Under the influence of the Soviet military administration, the Soviet occupation zone broke with the traditionally tripartite school system and established instead a uniform school system designed to provide eight years of standard education for all children. With the introduction of the polytechnical school (*Polytechnische Oberschule* or POS) in 1959, the transition to the "socialist school" was completed. The POS was based on compulsory schooling for 10 years followed by polytechnical education. Those who wanted to continue on the tertiary level of education at technical colleges or universities were required to complete their vocational training first (Anweiler et al. 1992:531).

After the Eighth Party Congress of the Socialist party in the spring of 1971, access to the universities was handled in a rather restrictive manner. In the 1980s only about 14 to 15 percent of an age cohort managed to qualify for university entrance (Fischer 1992:65). By arguing for more efficiency and higher productivity in society, the natural and technical sciences were extended at the expense of the humanities. Many high school graduates were excluded from entering university if they lacked the appropriate ideological orientation. Also, following the Soviet model, research was shifted to institutions outside the universities. In contrast to the idea of general universities, innumerable and highly specialized universities based upon a rather small range of subjects trained the future labor force for clearly defined jobs.

The East German socialist model of education, of course, came crashing down soon after the Berlin Wall in 1989. Once Germany was unified, and the Basic Law was extended to the former East Germany, within stages the West German model of education was extended to the East. As one can imagine, there have been problems of dislocation, loss of faculty jobs, and feelings of domination by the West in education as in other sectors of society being reorganized according to the western model. But given that education is one of the basic institutions of modern societies, if the two parts of Germany are to be unified in every respect, so must the system of education throughout Germany today.

Postwar Educational Expansion: More Opportunities, Less Justice?

One of the biggest and most important changes in Germany after World War II was the educational expansion of the 1960s and 1970s in West Germany. Many more secondary schools of all kinds and universities were built, with much more equal access for all Germans. Much of the educational expansion was motivated by the need for a better qualified labor force to continue economic expansion. But this educational expansion was also closely linked with political demands for more equality of opportunity, especially for children from working class families, for girls, and for children from the countryside (Dahrendorf 1965a; Geissler 1994:111–59).

Reform and expansion of education have had both positive and negative effects on society, however. In closing this section we briefly look at the effects on the educational system itself. At the secondary level, children from families with working class or lower middle class backgrounds have profited from the extension of the *Realschule*. The extension of the *Gymnasium* has mostly benefited those who were already among the privileged groups, that is, the children of civil servants, entrepreneurs, and white-collar workers. In competing for higher academic degrees, more children of working class origin than ever attend institutions of higher learning; however, with inflation of academic diplomas, they have lost ground compared to the other groups.

In the former GDR, the support for children of industrial and farm workers was designed to put an end to the middle class's monopoly on social ascent through education. The political elite was to be recruited from among all social classes. The goal to increase the proportion of university students with working class backgrounds had been achieved by preferential treatment of those who showed loyalty to the socialist regime. Children from the former middle classes, which were more critical of the communist system, suffered from state sanctions by being denied access to educational opportunities.

After 1958, when the educational privilege of the socialist intelligentsia had been established, the inequality of educational opportunities increased again. The social liberalization of the GDR in the first decade of its existence was followed by a period of social obstruction, eventually leading to the decline of the regime. In the final phase of the GDR, the social selection preceding enrollment at universities was even sharper than in West Germany. The proportion of working class children among the university student body was smaller than in West Germany; the number of children in the university student body whose parents held academic degrees was about twice as high.

CONCLUSION

To a large degree, the relative failure to achieve much equality of opportunity through education in Germany supports previous German beliefs. Because of its past experiences with feudalism and class conflicts, Germans, in contrast to Americans, do not fully believe that equality of opportunity is tantamount to the pursuit of happiness. Germany started out with the attempt to institutionalize the solution of the "social question" posed by the poor, the homeless, and the unemployed in the 19th century, and continued with the debate mainly led by Social Democrats, the labor movement, and some liberals through the 20th century. In effect, we can say Germans don't really believe equality of opportunity will work all that well, and in its place believe that there should be at least some "equality of results." This simply means that if material inequalities are seen as too great, which is to say, too many people are poor or income is distributed too unequally, then the state should step in with taxes and other policies to reduce such inequality.

This is one of the reasons the German "welfare state" is so much more extensive than in the United States. Though Germany has instituted almost complete and easy access to all schools, and universities with free tuition and stipends to some students for basic living costs while in a university, it is government policies and taxes that have been quite effective in making Germany a more equal society than the United States (Verba et al. 1987; Strasser 1973, 1974).

CHAPTER 8

Social Problems

One of America's most respected sociologists years ago made a distinction between "personal troubles of milieu" and "public issues of social structure" (Mills 1959:8–9). C. Wright Mills used the following example: "When, in a city of 100,000 only one man is unemployed, that is his personal trouble," but "when in a nation of 50 million employees, 15 million men are unemployed, that is a [public] issue." In the post–World War II era, Germany's rise from the ashes of destruction led many people to talk about the "German miracle." In recent years Germany has always been highly rated as the best country in the world to live. We have seen that the wages of German workers are the highest in the world, and their hours of work per week the lowest. Poverty, we have also seen, is very low by American standards. With the obvious exception of problems of racism suggested by Germany's past, would C. Wright Mills, therefore, have talked mostly about the personal troubles in Germany rather than the public issues—that is, the social problems?

With respect to a few of the social problems considered most serious in the United States, a few years ago the answer might often have been yes. But some conditions that won Germany the label of one of the most pleasant places to live a few years ago are growing sour. Various social problems are getting worse, and there is fear that they may become far worse in the future. Ironically, as we will see, some of the conditions that made Germany one of the best places to live have recently been blamed for creating growing social problems.

In this chapter we examine a standard set of social problems for Germany—poverty and unemployment, crime, racial discrimination, and population problems—while saving consideration of a few others more directly related to social change for our final chapter. Other problems, such as gender inequality, were already discussed in previous chapters.

UNEMPLOYMENT AND POVERTY

In the chapter on social stratification we saw that poverty hardly exists in Germany. For example, the percent of people with incomes at 40 percent or less of the average net income of the society (one measure of relative poverty), was only 3.6 percent of the German population in 1992 compared to about 25 percent for the United States (Hanesch et al. 1994:138; Parkes 1997:107). When measuring poverty by how much money is needed for basic necessities, as traditionally done by the US government, we find poverty rates as listed in Table 8–1. Compared to the United States, poverty is not such a significant social problem in Germany.

There is criticism that the estimates of poverty in Germany are inaccurate, and that the rate of *hidden poverty* is about 60 percent of all reported cases. If this estimate of hidden poverty is correct, the rate of poverty in Germany is almost 5 percent of the population instead of around 2.8 percent (Neumann 1995:80). Still, of course, the German rate of poverty is only a fraction of that in the United States.[16]

In another striking contrast between Germany and the United States, however, unemployment is a *big* social problem for Germany, but not so for the United States in the late 1990s. Not since the 1970s has the United States (even briefly) had an unemployment rate above 10 percent; in the second half of the 1990s the US unemployment rate has even been below 5 percent. Since 1992, the unemployment rate for Germany has been above 10 percent and as high as 12.6 percent (with many people estimating the "real" unemployment rate to be much higher).

Even these figures do not tell the whole story, however. In the western part of Germany the average unemployment rate was 9.4 percent in 1998, though in some regions such as the Ruhr area (the industrial heartland around Duisburg and Essen) it is up to 18 percent. But in the eastern part the unemployment rate averaged 18.2 percent in 1998, and in a number of old industrial regions of the East it exceeds even 30 percent. The overall unemployment for Germany was 11.1 percent in 1998. Experts estimate the real unemployment rate would be much higher if people were included who are in job creation programs, in training programs, in early retirement, or simply not looking actively for a job but willing to enter the labor market if there were more jobs.

Furthermore, a growing number of Germans who are out of work have been unemployed for many years, with no hope of finding stable work again. These people are called *long-term unemployed* if they are without a job for a year or more, presently some one-third of all unemployed. Most of the long-term unemployed are also considered "hardly employable" because of low skills, age, and/or health problems. In fact, the duration of unemployment often turns out to be *the* crucial obstacle to getting a job again because employers are often skeptical about hiring people who have been out of work so long (Strasser 1998).[17]

TABLE 8–1

Percentage of Population Living in Poverty, Major Industrial Nations: 1984–1987

Country	All Persons	Children
United States	13.3%	20.4%
Canada	7.0	9.3
Australia	6.7	9.0
United Kingdom	5.2	7.4
France	4.5	4.6
Netherlands	3.4	3.8
Germany	2.8	2.8
Sweden	4.3	1.6

Source: Adapted from Shapiro (1992:74), Smeeding (1991), Mishel and Bernstein (1993:434).

Unemployment, of course, is not only a German problem. Other countries in Europe such as Spain, Finland, Ireland, and Italy have dramatically higher levels of unemployment than Germany, with Spain beyond the 20 percent level. The people in these other European countries share pretty much the same characteristics of the unemployed in Germany: They are often less qualified, single parents, foreigners, suffering from health problems, disabled, and, of course, long-term unemployed. In the European Union (EU) as a whole, about 50 percent of the registered unemployed were without work for one year or longer and 30 percent for at least two years (European Commission 1997:35).

However, as shown in Figure 8–1, unemployment in the member states of the EU (shown as the E15 line in the graph) has continuously increased since the oil crisis of 1973–74. The EU unemployment rate is presently more than four times higher than in 1974. The lower part of Figure 8–1 shows that unemployment in the EU has gone up even though the percentage of the population who are of working age has stayed the same. For both the United States and Japan the opposite is true (60 and 74 percent, respectively, in 1996), and unemployment would have been much higher in the United States and Japan if they had not been creating so many new jobs. Thus, in the United States the number of jobs has considerably increased, with earnings remaining more or less the same in the last two decades; in Germany the average earnings have gone up but not the number of jobs.

In the eastern part of Germany, an entire generation is actually affected by long-term unemployment. In 1997, 4 out of 10 unemployed East Germans were looking for a job for more than four years, and al-

FIGURE 8-1

Unemployment Rates and Age Distribution in the European Union, the United States, and Japan, 1974–1996

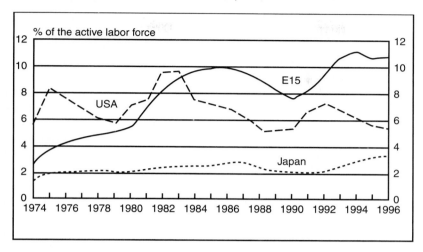

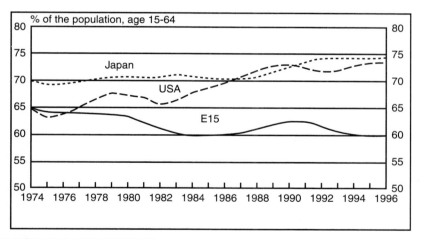

Source: European Commission (1997:28, 27).

most 5 out of 10 were unemployed between one and four years (Hanesch et al. 1994:37). Those who are presently between 45 and 65 years of age, encompassing almost one-third of the population, may therefore be regarded as East Germany's "lost generation." They are mostly too young to retire and too old for a new start (Geissler 1995b:121).

Unemployment versus Poverty

Following American assumptions about the subject one can make another set of puzzling observations. Germany has one of the lowest poverty rates in the world, but one of the highest unemployment rates of industrial nations. The United States, in contrast, has one of the lowest unemployment rates among industrial nations, but by far the highest poverty rate. At first this situation seems not to make sense; however, following the political and economic logic of what is happening it makes perfect sense.

Quite simply, Germany has low poverty in the face of high unemployment because unemployment benefits and welfare benefits are extensive enough to keep German people out of poverty even if they are unemployed. In contrast, wages are often so low in the United States that people working full time can fall into poverty. Furthermore, US welfare and unemployment benefits are very meager compared to those in Germany; even when they can be obtained by the poor in America, these benefits are not enough to bring them out of poverty. During the mid-1990s in the United States, for example, the Census Bureau estimated that 18 percent of all full-time workers fell below the poverty line (Kerbo 1996:271). This means people working 40 hours a week even above the set minimum wage. Even before the massive welfare cuts of the mid-1990s in the United States, average welfare benefits did not bring people above the poverty line. As noted above, in contrast to Germany, the US economy has produced many new jobs in recent decades. However, over 50 percent of the jobs created in the 1980s, and almost as many in the 1990s, paid wages below the poverty line (Harrison and Bluestone 1988; Kerbo 1996:271).

Next, one needs to ask, why does Germany have so much unemployment with a relatively strong economy? The answer to this question points to a difficult dilemma for countries such as Germany. Unemployment is high, in large measure, because wages, benefits, and unemployment payments are so high. For example, as we have seen, German wages are among the highest in the world, and in addition to this, employers must pay another 41 to 84 percent to cover health, social security, and other benefits for workers, compared to only 29 percent for US benefits (Mertes 1996:12). As shown in Figure 8–2, while in Germany wages are high and the employment rate is low, in the United States the opposite is true. German labor costs were some 80 percent above the US level in 1995 (Strasser 1997b:19–20). Also, with German labor laws, as we have seen, it is very difficult to fire workers, again making employers cautious about hiring new employees. This means that it is very expensive for German employers to hire new workers, and consequently they would rather make do with the ones they have. Finally, extensive welfare benefits tend to make potential workers less likely to take jobs at low wages. Through the 20th century, among all industrial nations, more extensive welfare and unemployment benefits have provided support and bargain-

FIGURE 8–2

Employment and Wages in Germany and the United States, 1970–1995

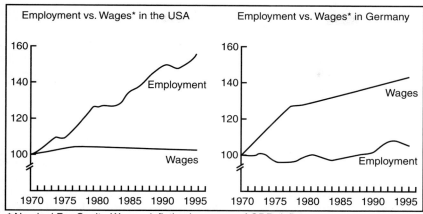

* Nominal Per-Capita-Wages deflation by means of GDP-deflators

Source: Strasser (1997a:20).

ing power for workers (Piven and Cloward 1982). Workers, in other words, are not so desperate as to take jobs with wages that are below the poverty line. Extensive welfare and unemployment benefits in fact help those who are employed because of the pressure on employers to keep wages higher than welfare benefits to attract and keep good workers.

In short, the very things that keep poverty and inequality low in a society can also help keep unemployment rather high. There is, thus, a dilemma or a trade-off: A country can have relatively high unemployment in part due to generous welfare benefits and laws giving extensive rights to workers (but with the positive effects of relatively low poverty and inequality), or a country can have low unemployment but high poverty and inequality. A few countries have been able to have high wages and benefits without extensive unemployment protection and welfare coverage, such as Japan, but these countries indeed have been few (Kerbo 1996:466–69).

Which side of the dilemma a country chooses often depends upon two things: national values favoring more or less inequality and the power of workers. Germany, we have seen, values low inequality in the post–World War II period, and German workers certainly are among the most powerful in the industrial world. Today we sometimes hear Germany described as having a "Rhenish economy" to distinguish it from that of the United States, which is in many ways the opposite.

Before turning from this subject we note an often-stated fear among Germans today: The number of people currently unemployed comes close to the number unemployed in the early 1930s, a number that fueled the despair and political discontent leading to the rise of Hitler. There are, however, at least two big differences between the 1930s and the present. First, the unemployed in Germany today are supported by one of the most solid welfare systems in the world. While unemployment might create psychological depression, there is seldom fear of poverty for Germans of the 1990s. Second, as we have seen, and will consider further, despite high unemployment, the German economy is surprisingly strong. Restructuring in the face of globalization could make the German economy even stronger in the next few decades.

CRIME AND VICE

Germany's criminal justice system adheres to principles similar to those of most other industrial nations. There are defense attorneys and public prosecutors, courts with judges (and like most of the rest of the world, very few trials with juries made up of citizens as in the United States), and of course police officers and prisons. Also like most of the industrialized world, and in contrast to the United States, in Germany there are relatively few prisoners (all European nations and Japan have less than 100 people per 100,000 population behind bars, while the United States is number one in the world with over 400). There are few hand guns (only 6 percent of the population have one compared to almost 30 percent in the United States), and there is no death penalty (Shapiro 1992).

Considering the above, and also considering Germany's reputation for order and respect for authority, one could accurately predict that the German crime rate is relatively low, or at least more in line with crime rates in other European nations and far below the US crime rate. Further, knowing that there is usually some relationship between high income inequality and higher crime, we would also expect that crime is a relatively small problem in Germany (Blau and Blau 1982; Williams 1984).

Crime Rate

Crime statistics from different countries are difficult to compare due to differences in reporting and defining crime. Crime victimization surveys, which ask a sample of the population if they have been a crime victim in the past year, are somewhat more reliable; these indicate the US crime rate is the highest while Germany's is lower and close to that of other European nations (Shapiro 1992:118). Statistics for violent crime, and especially murder, however, are a more reliable means of comparison. As can be seen in Table 8–2, the German murder rate is close to the range of most other industrial nations at 4.2 per 100,000 population, and far below the US top position of almost 10 per 100,000 population. The biggest difference between the murder rate in for the United States and in other in-

TABLE 8–2

Comparative Murder Rates*

Country	Murder Rate† Overall	Males 15–24 Years Old
United States	9.4	21.9
Sweden	7.2	2.3
Canada	5.5	2.9
Denmark	5.2	1.0
France	4.6	1.4
Australia	4.5	2.5
Germany	4.2	1.0
Belgium	2.8	1.7
Switzerland	2.3	1.4
Italy	2.2	Nd
England	2.0	1.2
Austria	1.8	Nd
Japan	1.0	0.5

*Data are for the late 1980s to 1990.
†Rates per 100,000 population.
Source: Data from Shapiro (1992).

dustrial nations is located on the right side of Table 8–2: The United States had more than 20 murders per 100,000 population among young males, compared to 1 to 2 or less for the other industrial nations.

Even at a much lower rate than the United States, however, the crime rate in Germany is not acceptable to Germans, and certainly defined as a social problem. More importantly, though, the German crime rate has been rising significantly in recent years and has Germans worried. Between 1994 and 1996, for example, the crime rate jumped by 15 percent. There is no solid evidence yet as to why the German crime rate has been increasing, but there are some likely causes. Following standard reasons for rising crime in other industrial nations, and despite the overall low level of inequality in Germany, the high level of unemployment and a large influx of relatively poor Eastern Europeans after the fall of communism are usually cited as reasons for Germany's growing crime rate. As is common, and as noted by one of the sociological masters, Émile Durkheim, increases in deviance such as crime usually accompany other social problems (such as unemployment) and social change. Until the problems facing Germany in adjusting to a new world economy and change among its neighbor nations are sorted out, we might expect the German crime rate to continue its rise in the near future.

Sexual Offenses

We again invoke the ideas of the sociological master Durkheim that all societies have their vices; how much, and, perhaps more interestingly, what is considered a vice (or deviance) in one society compared to another, can tell us quite a lot about a society. In this regard, the traditional social problems of prostitution and drug use are instructive when comparing Germany to the United States.

With respect to prostitution, Germany has it, but it is legal, and rather well regulated. Most northwestern European countries in general are less uptight about sex and nudity than are Americans (which is one reason Americans are often startled when going to swimming pools for the first time in Germany), and have legalized prostitution. The attitude is simply that prostitution is an age-old "institution" that cannot be eliminated, so one might as well allow it but regulate it to limit as much as possible potential abuses. Thus, in many German cities there are "red light districts" (an extremely large and notorious one is in Hamburg) where women (and some men) work openly to find customers. Police patrol these areas to help protect all involved, and health workers try to keep the prostitutes healthy and well informed about sexually transmitted illnesses. (Which makes it interesting to note that AIDS and HIV are relatively rare in Germany compared to the United States.)

The sex industry in Germany, however, is not without growing problems. Most troubling to Germans, and Europeans in general, is the increasing number of poor young women coming to rich European countries such as Germany, at times held as virtual sex slaves by organized crime groups. Recent estimates are that some 200,000 to 500,000 young women are now in the richer European countries working as prostitutes. While a small percentage of these women are held against their will, the exact number is unclear (*The European*, Nov. 21, 1996; April 17 and June 13, 1997).

Another troubling aspect of prostitution involves "sex tours" organized for German men to a few Southeast Asian nations such as Thailand where the sexual abuse of young women and men is much easier to get away with. In Thailand there are likely 10,000 young girls held against their will (or tricked into becoming prostitutes), a large percentage in their early teenage years (estimates by UNICEF; see, for example, *Bangkok Post*, August 28 and Nov. 24, 1997). Thailand's nongovernmental welfare organizations (NGOs) estimate that Germany, Switzerland, Sweden, and Japan are the countries where most sex tour groups to Thailand originate. There has been some success in European nations such as Germany with new laws that make it illegal to have sex with minors outside of the country; a few men have been arrested and brought back for prosecution in recent years.

Drug Abuse

Drug abuse also makes for an interesting comparison between Germany and the United States. In Germany illegal drugs, divided into soft (e.g., cannabis) and hard drugs (e.g., opiates, hallucinogens, amphetamines), are less accepted and are dealt with by the police more harshly than in neighboring countries such as the Netherlands. While the problem is much less severe in Germany than in the United States, it has developed into a major issue on both the individual and political levels. There are a few places, such as the vicinity of the central railway station in large cities, where drug addicts and sellers are openly active, though the tendency is to withdraw to hidden private quarters.

Currently there is much controversy in Germany over what policies are best in dealing with drug abuse. Conservatives, including the Christian Democrats, favor an abstinence strategy that aims at a controlled use of legal drugs such as alcohol, nicotine, and medical drugs, on the one hand, and prohibiting the use of illegal drugs (whether soft or hard), on the other. Their key words are "fighting drug use" that is "endangering social order." Their counterparts, the liberals, argue for "preventing addiction" and avoiding the "consequences of criminalizing drug use." The liberals, including large numbers of the now-governing Social Democrats and the Green Party, advocate the acceptance strategy of liberalizing soft drugs and controlling the distribution of hard drugs to heavily addicted persons, thus focusing on coming to terms with the consequences of drug use (Strasser and Boumans 1996). While the former seem to fear more consumption and more users (and these could be one's own children), the latter are troubled by the vicious circle of drug abuse and criminalization, addiction, and provision crime. The conservatives tend to look at what happens before someone is a drug abuser; the liberals prefer to see what happens after someone uses drugs (such as turning to crime in order to pay for the drug addiction).

The controversy heated up in December 1990 when representatives of all political parties and major organizations met with then Chancellor Kohl to launch a fight against drug abuse, the National Drug Prevention Plan—almost 10 years after President Reagan had declared a "war on drugs" in the United States. Since then, the number of users of hard core drugs has almost tripled; the official count of addicts is at 150,000, while "real" estimates go as high as 200,000 to 300,000. In the same period, the number of people who have used hard drugs for the first time has increased by more than 50 percent; these figures had quadrupled between 1983 and 1993. The number of newcomers to the hard drug scene reaches new record highs every year. The highest growth rates are for users of hallucinogens such as LSD and pep pills such as ecstasy and speed, followed by cocaine. Heroin use stagnates at a high level. Presently, about

50 percent of those who use hard drugs for the first time do so with synthetic drugs.

Naturally, police seizures of drugs and the number of drug offenses mirror these developments closely, although the police seize only a very small amount of the drugs available (probably not more than 10 percent). Moreover, cannabis products such as hashish and marijuana are no longer seized in large quantities. This, of course, is not tantamount to a decline in consumption but rather an indication of their quasi-legalization, which not even the police can avoid. It is estimated that there are some 6 million Germans under 40 years of age who have at least tried soft drugs (i.e., about every third youth), though most of them stop after the first time. The proportion of users who use drugs on a regular basis over a longer period of time ranges between 18 and 20 percent of all persons with hashish experience. This amounts to approximately 1 million compared to some 10 million cannabis users in the United States, as reported by the United Nations' International Narcotics Control Board for 1996 (United Nations 1997). The only good news is, however, that the number of fatal drug victims has been slowly decreasing—with peaks of more than 2,000 at the beginning of the 1990s and 1,501 in 1997.

Beneath the surface of these quantative changes, Germany has witnessed a more fundamental change in drug consumption. The number of heroin users has seemingly declined, because some of them withdraw to the invisible private sphere, while activating drugs such as cocaine, amphetamines, LSD, and ecstasy are booming. Marijuana and hashish have enjoyed a renaissance. Cocaine is increasingly accepted by users of all status groups (though crack is not as widespread as in the United States), and with the rhythm of techno and cyberspace, the market for designer drugs is exploding. These happy pills seem to go along with the spirit of the age more than such "hippie drugs" as marijuana and hashish. As confirmed time and again by drug researchers, it seems to be "out" for young Germans to be stunned and "in" to be stimulated. The consumption of drugs has become an individual pastime rather than a collective experience (Strasser and Boumans 1996).

Most of these drugs come from neighboring Holland by way of the so-called ants traffic over the open border, much to the chagrin of German authorities. Moreover, differences between national drug control policies, as well as the ongoing discussion about the liberalization or legalization of the nonmedical use of drugs threaten the consensus needed for concerted actions against drug abuse and drug trafficking. Indeed, the differences in dealing with the drug problem could not be greater. The only common denominator seems to be the firm stand against drugs on the part of the European Commission; most international organizations are against drug abuse and drug trafficking, while national governments take a more differentiated and less firm position (see, e.g., United Nations 1997).

Most German youth begin using drugs nowadays between 13 and 15 years of age with alcohol and cannabis and change between ages 16 and 18 to ecstasy. In this respect there is almost no difference between East and West Germany, though hard drugs are still less used in the East. It is estimated that some 4 million youths have at least tried ecstasy once in the past 10 years. Estimates also indicate that 4 to 5 percent of cannabis users change later to heroin. To put it statistically another way, 96 percent of all users of hard drugs have started out with cannabis. Nevertheless, alcohol is still the main entrance drug among German youngsters, and if there is a drug problem in German schools, it has to do with alcohol. It is also striking that young people increasingly take prescribed and over-the-counter drugs and more often use several drugs at the same time (e.g., alcohol, cannabis, and prescribed or over-the-counter drugs).

According to the German Agency Against Drug Addiction (*Deutsche Hauptstelle gegen Suchtgefahren* or *DHS*), there are some 2.5 million Germans considered alcoholics, about 6 million tobacco smokers in need of treatment, and 1.4 million hooked on medication. Germans are also world champions at drinking alcohol (during 1994 consuming 11.4 liters of pure alcohol per inhabitant, that is, 17.5 liters of wine and 139.6 liters of beer per person). This seems to mirror the permissive-dysfunctional culture of drinking, which not only tolerates drinking but also expects even excessive drinking in certain circumstances (Schweer 1997; Pittman 1967).

Despite all the efforts of the past years, the goal to reduce drug use so far has been failed. The use of state force and the criminalization of the market have not brought about any encouraging results, nor have the alternative experiments with drug substitutes, treatment programs, and public drug injection rooms on the state and community levels. The Swiss model of providing addicts with heroin in a controlled way has been rejected thus far. The present German government has already announced that it will follow a liberal stance and focus on medical treatment and psycho-social care of addicts as well as intensified instruction of parents, children, teachers, and friends. Although most Germans would go along with the American concept of "community policing" as a systematic attempt to reduce the crime rate, "political correctness" has not yet permitted its implementation on a larger scale. In Germany today, the strategy of "minimizing the social costs" by influencing the form of the drug market on a societal level and of "harm reduction" on the individual level is the name of the game (Kaiser 1996:182). To many critics this is the ultimate surrender to drug abuse and the drug mafia.

RACE AND ETHNIC DISCRIMINATION

When the subject of racial and ethnic discrimination comes up, most people around the world still think of Germany: As we have already discussed, the Nazi legacy and the extermination of six million people, mostly Jews, will not be forgotten for many generations, if ever. It is difficult, however, to make a case that something in the German psyche explains racism among Germans.

In fact, a poll of 16,000 people in 15 European countries sponsored by the European Union (EU) in 1997 found that Germans today were less racist in their attitudes than people in Belgium, France, and Austria where 22 percent, 16 percent, and 14 percent, respectively, admitted to being "quite racist or very racist" (*International Herald Tribune*, December 20, 1997). It could well be that because of their past, Germans are more cautious about admitting racism. However, the data do show a dangerously high amount of racism throughout many European countries today, with anti-immigrant and at least mildly racist political candidates gaining more support all over Europe. It must be pointed out that Germans not only express less racism in opinion polls today, they also are less likely to vote for candidates who can be described as having racist overtones. Only 2 percent of Germans have voted for far-right, antiforeigner political parties in recent years, much less than in many other European countries, especially neighboring France (*International Herald Tribune*, June 24, 1997).

Whatever the attitudes of most Germans, however, there continue to be many problems in Germany related to racial and ethnic conflicts. In Germany, a considerable number of attacks on foreigners occurred in the early 1990s, though these attacks have now dropped dramatically (Parkes 1997:67). According to the official statistics of the German Office for the Protection of the Constitution and the Federal Department of the Interior, these attacks peaked at 2,639 in 1992, were at 781 in 1996, and slightly increased again in 1997 (*International Herald Tribune*, January 24, 1998; Backes 1997). As was suggested by the EU, it seems anger toward foreigners is also a class issue; foreigners are not only alien but also competitors for jobs.[18]

The Office for the Protection of the Constitution in Germany counted 96 right-wing organizations at the end of 1995. Membership is decreasing but the number of people who readily use violent means has gone up. Among these organizations one finds such nationalist political parties as the *Republikaner*, but also groups of right-wing skinheads whose forms of protest range from subcultural consumer products (rock music, computer games, videos) to discriminating actions against foreigners, especially in the eastern part of Germany. There is some indication that East German youth are less able to deal with disappointments and stress, which could explain why they turn their protest outside in terms of vandalism against things and people (Schmidtchen 1997:344). Other observers suspect that the right-wing youth protest might even develop into a social movement (Jaschke 1994:10).

The underlying problems, of course, are the high rate of unemployment throughout most of Europe (unemployment often higher than the 11 percent found in Germany, and as high as 25 percent in some eastern parts of Germany), the irritating pace of change, and the large influx of immigrants throughout Europe with the fall of communist governments

Among many official attempts to promote ethnic integration, the German Soccer Association arranged a soccer match between the German national team and a team recruited from the best foreign players in the German Federal Soccer League. The photo shows young Germans and Turks carrying Turkish and German flags, which is also very symbolic for the current debate over whether young Turks who were born in Germany should receive German citizenship and be able to retain their Turkish passport.

in Eastern Europe at the end of the 1980s. During the early 1990s, for example, Germany had almost half a million immigrants every year. The above-mentioned poll on racist attitudes by the European Union, as expected, found that people who were unemployed or feared unemployment were most likely to admit to racist beliefs, and overall in Europe, 43 percent of people said even legal immigrants from outside of the European Union should be sent home.

Even though migration to Germany has multiplied since the late 1950s, less than 10 percent of the German population are foreign born and some 11 percent or 8.5 million are presently considered foreigners (Parkes 1997:103; Strasser 1997a). It is true that this is a higher percentage of foreign-born people living in Germany than in the United States, where just over 9 percent of the 265 million US residents were foreign born in 1996 (Strasser 1997a). However, of all US-born residents in the United States, a much greater percentage are from some racial or ethnic minority than are German residents. Of all citizens or legal residents in Germany, over 95 percent are completely of German heritage, and 3 percent are of Turkish background, the largest group of foreigners who had come to Germany as guest workers between the 1950s and 1970s.

In contrast to the United States, German nationalism and identity are based upon supposed qualities of blood, ancestry, and language.

In the United States, for example, one can be American but have ancestors who were French, Japanese, Chinese, Mexican, African, or whatever. In Germany, by contrast, there are about 2.5 million people of Turkish ancestry, many living in Germany for two or three generations, but few have been allowed German citizenship. About 60 percent of them have lived 10 or more years in West Germany. The former GDR hosted, besides 380,000 Soviet soldiers plus their 200,000 family members, close to 200,000 foreigners or 1 percent of the residential population, mostly people from Vietnam, Mozambique, Cuba, Poland, Angola, and China (Dicke 1993). On the other hand, German law gives instant citizenship to people such as the few hundred thousand living in Russia whose parents left Germany 200 years ago.

Rather than suggesting that racist attitudes or even the exclusion of other ethnic groups from German nationality are a result of some psychological aversion or innate racism, it is best understood as an underlying aspect of German social structure. Compared to most other industrial societies, and particularly to the United States, Germany has historically been a rather homogenous society with respect to race and ethnicity. Like Japan, throughout German history there were few "non-Germans," as defined by a long ancestry, living in the territory. Unlike France, England, and the Netherlands, for example, Germany did not have a long history of colonialism that brought many people from around the world to live in the country, nor has Germany the same traditions as a country of immigrants as the United States.[19]

Thus, as sociological masters have shown us, from Simmel (1905) to Coser (1956, 1967), a greater sense of in-group homogeneity produces a stronger sense of an out-group in the society. Some historians have also suggested that we must realize that Germany, as we know it today, is a relatively young country, having experienced its first unification in the late 1800s, and that Germany still has fewer symbols of national identity than most other countries (Parkes 1997:181). Germans have no July 14 like the French, or 4th of July like the Americans, or major events of symbolic significance to invoke national identity other than German ancestry. Its national holiday, the 3rd of October, commemorating the reunification, is of very recent origin, as had been its predecessor, June 17, reminding Germans of the brave workers in East Germany who rebelled against the totalitarian Soviet-supported regime in 1953. Moreoover, the social and political transformations have been too many to generate unanimous grounds for identification. It will take some time before the focus on "German blood" as an identifying characteristic will become secondary and eventually irrelevant in Germany.

POPULATION PROBLEMS

Several advanced industrial societies are experiencing some type of population problem, but, with the exception of Japan, few other countries are in a more difficult position than is Germany. Sociologists in the field of **demography** are in the business of tracking and predicting several types of population changes, such as migrations, birth rates, death rates, age distributions, and, of course, overall population growth (or declines).

In short, the basic problem for Germany now, and more so in the future, is too many elderly people and too few babies. This means that there are more and more older people to support with fewer workers, and even fewer workers in the future because of a "baby bust." Without other changes, like more immigration, the problem of too few babies means population decline. At its extreme, and if present rates continue for a couple of centuries, there could be no Germans left (as Germans tend to define being German by national ancestry).

To explain the problem we start with the baby deficit, which comes from the fact that fewer and fewer women are having children in Germany today. Currently the average family in Germany has 1.26 children compared to 2.1 for the United States. To maintain a steady population size, the average number of children per woman of reproductive age should at least be 2.1. Another figure showing the baby bust in Germany is the **crude birth rate,** or the number of births each year per 1,000 people in the society. In the mid-1990s, this crude birth rate in the United States was over 15, while it was just over 10 for Germany.

Reasons for having fewer children are of course complex, and include such things as the increased costs of having children, more opportunities for women to do things other than stay home and raise children, and women's discontent with current situations (with family life and/or the country in general). There are increasing opportunities for women in Germany, as we have seen in the chapter on social stratification. However, German women still lag behind many countries with respect to occupational opportunities; thus, this should not be a primary cause of low fertility. The disincentives for having children could also be due to the high unemployment rate in Germany; again this explanation must be incomplete because the baby bust predated the currently high unemployment rates. More likely is that the decline in having children is connected with why German women are less likely to get married (or marry later) today than in the past and are discontent with current gender roles. Many studies and experience show a growing disparity between the attitudes of men and women toward gender roles and family in Germany (Davis and Robinson 1991).

Some of the growing discontent among younger German women is reflected in other figures: Divorce in Germany is on the rise, and 70 percent of divorces are instituted by women rather than men; over 35 percent of German households are now led by singles, and about 30 percent of women between 18 and 65 in Germany are unmarried (Hoffmeister and Tubach 1992:187). It is interesting to add at this point that in the former East Germany the marriage rate and birth rate were much higher, and more in line with other industrial nations. Since the reunification of East Germany and West Germany, however, the eastern rates of marriage and child birth have been dropping toward the level of western Germany (Parkes 1997:100).

The other major population problem in Germany is an aging population. Currently about 16 percent of the German population is over 65 compared to 12 percent in the United States; in 20 years that rate for Germany will be 25 percent over 65, compared to only a slight increase for the United States. Part of the cause of the aging population is certainly a positive one: People are living longer. About 100 years ago the average life expectancy in Germany was only 45; today, it is close to 77 years. But the other side of the cause is again the baby bust: The percentage of the population over 65 is affected by the dropping percentage of the population under 15.

The simple reason that an aging population is a problem comes from the required care of the older population—both economically and socially. People over 65 are most often not contributing to economic production. Back when Bismarck created the German social security system life expectancy was 45 years and there were many workers putting money into the social security system to take care of each elderly person. Today, it takes three workers being taxed at 19 percent of their wages to take care of each elderly person in Germany, while by 2020 each worker will need to be taxed 35 percent to take care of only one retired German each (Mertes 1996:13).

Germany is faced with difficult questions related to the currently generous social security and medical care systems. Much more than the United States, Germany must either increase taxes (now up to 50 percent of wages) on the active labor force to help support the higher percentage of elderly in the future, or must cut health and social security benefits, or some combination of the two. As in the United States, the elderly tend to be an important political interest group, so cutting their benefits will not be easy. But on the other hand, to remain competitive in the new world economy and to conform to the rigid unification guidelines of the European Union, taxes and government spending must come down. Like most other European countries, these dilemmas are likely to produce higher levels of political discontent among the population in coming years.

URBAN PROBLEMS: SUBURBANIZATION AS A SOCIAL PROBLEM

We conclude this chapter with what may seem strange to Americans to include as a social problem—suburbanization. We examine this social problem to drive home the point that *value choices* are often behind what comes to be defined as a social problem and what does not.

By *suburbanization,* of course, we mean the common US phenomenon of people moving their residences from the cities to suburban areas, or residential communities away from, but close to larger cities. In contrast to Europeans, Americans have tended to view big cities as less inviting, to be avoided for the open spaces, and perhaps even as evil places full of crime, poverty, and other problems. Pioneering American sociologists at the University of Chicago during the early part of the 20th century, in fact, held this type of bias toward cities as well (Palen 1981). Following the standard pattern of American cities such as Chicago, early American sociologists such as Burgess (1925) created the model of concentric zones in which they assumed all cities would tend toward having a factory zone and low-income housing in the center of the city, with middle class residential zones moving further and further away from this central area over time. More commuter highways, automobiles, and shopping malls, of course, would follow these people to the outer zones of the cities, while the central areas would further deteriorate.

When looking around the world, however, we find these early American sociologists were not so accurate, and in many cases even wrong. Some of these patterns can be found in cities throughout Europe and Asia, for example, but much less so than in the United States. Europeans, and Germans especially, have had much more favorable attitudes toward cities, respecting them for their value as cultural centers, and for bringing people together. Driving through the German countryside one also sees a pattern quite different from the United States: There are almost no isolated farm houses anywhere through the countryside, but rather small little villages of 10, 20, or more farm families in a little cluster. Throughout history these people have preferred to live close to one another, and to drive out each morning to work in the fields, with practically no incidents of abandoning these villages and hamlets to become ghost towns.

There is some suburbanization occurring in Germany, however. Many Germans are worried that it may increase and erode the prized urban areas, bringing with it more autos, highways, and shopping malls. Germany has the lowest number of shopping malls for an industrialized country in Europe or North America. However, just between 1990 and 1995, the number of shopping malls in all of Germany increased from 90 to 204—compared to 40,000 shopping malls in the United States. Consequently, German politicians are currently debating new laws that can slow, if not stop, the growth of these shopping malls, and do other things that continue to make the central cities the attractive places for living, shopping, and centers of culture they have been throughout history.

CONCLUSION

Before concluding we must note that defining social problems is no simple task. One country's social problems can be another's accepted or even valued state of affairs. What comes to be defined as a social problem depends, therefore, to a large extent upon what people in the society value. This is also to say that one can tell much about a society by what that society does or does not define as a social problem.

One key value difference we can understand from this chapter is that Germans today are much more concerned about high levels of economic inequality than are Americans. They are less concerned about what Americans call *big government,* and they support welfare programs to reduce high inequality and poverty. On the other hand, much more experience with a multiracial and multiethnic society has led more Americans to accept diversity than Germans. This is *not* to say there are few problems of racism and discrimination in the United States. It is to say that the greater acceptance of diversity, with citizenship *not* so much defined in racial and ethnic terms as in Germany, has made racism and discrimination lower in the United States.

Social Change in the New Century

German Transitions and Post–Cold War Realities

On November 9, 1989, the world marveled at one of the most amazing scenes in history. It all began to unfold a few weeks before when Poland defied the Soviet Union as they had many times before. This time they allowed an anticommunist labor union to again exist (Solidarity); then they accepted the election of their first noncommunist prime minister in August 1989. At the time, the world again held its breath waiting for the Soviet tanks to roll in, crushing freedom and killing thousands as had happened in East Germany in 1953, in Hungary in 1956, and in Czechoslovakia in 1968. But a strange thing happened: The tanks did not move. New Soviet leader, Mikhail Gorbachev, decided to reverse Soviet policy.

Within days, people all over Eastern Europe responded to the "shot not heard around the world" by taking dramatic action. In communist East Germany, the old leaders tried to remain authoritative. As if nothing had happened they assured themselves, and the people at first, that they were still in charge. But when neighboring Hungary took anticommunist action by allowing East Germans to drive through their country to Austria and then on to Western Germany, the communist East German leaders were doomed. CNN brought us dramatic pictures of thousands of East Germans in their little cars packed with their possessions, all driving through checkpoints into West Germany, with Hungarian border guards smiling, wishing them good luck, and waving them on. In September 1989, 55,000 East Germans simply drove out; in October another 21,000 drove out (Eisel 1996:169–70). By November the old communist government in East Germany had lost its authority, while the participants at the so-called Monday demonstrations in Leipzig and other places claimed new authority: "We are the people." On November 9, 1989, East Germans decided the drive through Hungary was no longer necessary. They took matters into their own hands to give the world the most amazing TV pictures of all: Thousands of East Germans on one side of the Berlin Wall and thousands of West Berliners on the other side simply started tearing down that wall piece by piece with hammers. Then they all rushed through to embrace each other as whole sections of the wall began to fall. East German soldiers ripped off their communist insignia and threw them on the ground and joined the people. East Germany, in one sense, was gone overnight.

According to the law, finally enacted by the West German government, on October 3, 1990, both West Germany and East Germany ceased to exist; foreigners now sending letters to their friends in either the old West Germany or old East Germany could now simply finish the address, Germany. Thus began one of the unifications to profoundly affect Germany in the last decade of the 20th century. The other was moving more slowly, but also picked up steam as the 1990s progressed: Europe in general was moving toward another type of unification that would include Germany.

As the sociological masters were among the first to document, social change is a complex process. Parts of society react to each other in problematic ways, no doubt producing many benefits for the society at times, but also producing social problems. Some of these problems and changes are part and parcel of Germany's development of the past three or four hundred years. In spite of its slow unification between the 17th and 19th centuries and its late industrialization, the Prusso-Protestant virtues of order, diligence, and parsimoniousness in combination with the authoritarian state contributed to the development of an achievement society. After failing twice to gain world power in the 20th century, this achievement orientation led to the economic miracle of the past decades.

However, with the reunification of Germany in 1990 these prosperous conditions seem to have gone, as new technologies point to new limits on growth by doing away with jobs, increasing unemployment, and straining the welfare state. The German-style achievement society has maneuvered itself into a serious crisis, while the graying of the German population poses another, perhaps even more serious, challenge in the long run. Christian Graf von Krockow, a political scientist, has even observed the "German decline" (Krockow 1998). He argues that Germany has aging and employment problems. In addition he claims that hoping for a service miracle is in vain as long as Germany does not effectively deal with the following problems: the catastrophe of its educational system, especially the universities; the credibility crisis between the politicians and the governed; the reconstruction of the tax and welfare system; and the mobilization of the intellectual forces.

In the context of the societal changes brought on by the two unifications of Germany, there is, however, more to look at. The changes within the old Soviet Union that allowed the Berlin Wall to fall in the first place also set off ever-growing changes in the modern world system. With no longer a superpower conflict between the United States and the Soviet Union, a conflict that included people and nations in one way or another all over the world, the rules of the modern world system began to change. This subject, and its effect upon German society in the 1990s and beyond, must also be considered in this chapter.

GERMAN UNIFICATION AND ITS CONSEQUENCES

The flood of East Germans moving to the West before the wall went down did not stop on November 9. They kept coming across the old East-West border in ever greater numbers. In November some 157,000, mostly young people looking for new careers and a better life, came to the West with all their belongings; in December 54,000 moved, followed by 74,000 in January, 64,000 in February, and 46,000 in March (Eisel 1996:170). Already by December East Germans were marching in demonstrations with banners reading "If the deutsche mark does not come to us, then we will go to it!" The joke at the time was that German unification would take place in an unexpected way—all East Germans would move to the West. The West German government, obviously, had to act quickly to prepare the political ground for formal unification and to create economic opportunities for the former East Germans at home before they all moved west.

Political Unification

Political unification was by far the least difficult problem to solve, though even here serious problems arose. The West German constitution created after World War II, the Basic Law, contained provisions for unifying Germany again. It stated that either East Germany could simply be brought under the West German governmental authority, much like was done during the early history of the United States by accepting new states to the Union; or, the people of both eastern and western Germany could vote on a new constitution, after the long process of writing and deciding on what the people would have to vote had taken place, of course. With the urgency of the situation described, the German government understandably took the first option. As of October 3, 1990, the provinces of the former East Germany were integrated as new *Laender* into the existing authorities of the Federal Republic of Germany under the Basic Law (Kocka 1996:195). These new *Laender* in the unified Germany elected their representatives to the central German government, followed the Basic Law in electing their own new state governments, and applied all other laws—from the criminal justice system to social security and education—to themselves. Finally, in a symbolic act of great complexity, representatives of the new unified Germany voted to move the national capital back to Berlin from Bonn, which had become the provisional capital of West Germany soon after World War II. This not only signified the new Germany but also moved geopolitically closer to the East. As much as Bonn was not Weimar, neither will Berlin be Bonn.

Social and Psychological Unification

The political party alignments and competition for new voters need not concern us here. We do need to note that eventually, when the euphoria of the united Germany faded to the new realities, there was growing resentment by former East Germans over many issues. Former East Germans came to feel they were being colonized by the West rather than Germany being unified. Nothing that existed in their previous collective lives seemed to be of any value in the new Germany; the official name of the former West Germany (the Federal Republic of Germany) remained, the flag and the national hymn were the same, and most things in the East were made to fit what the West thought was best. For example, the university system in the old East Germany, which had been modeled after the old Soviet system of separate universities for particular functions (e.g., universities to train teachers, others to train technical specialists such as engineers, and still others to train government administrators) was changed to the Western model of integrated universities. Further, professors from the West came to take over the top positions. For example, of the 29 top professors of sociology in East German universities in the mid-1990s, only 4 were East Germans (Kocka 1996:201).

Resentments and conflicts developed in many spheres of life. West Germans tended to look down upon the "Ossies" (Easties) as being lazy and less sophisticated; the East Germans looked down upon the "Wessies" (Westies) as materialistic, greedy, and arrogant. By 1993 opinion polls showed the divisions; only 22 percent of West Germans and 11 percent of East Germans felt "together, like Germans" (Winkler 1996:69). Further, 71 percent of West Germans and 85 percent of East Germans felt they were "divided by opposing interests."

We must understand that what underlies this division is one of the most interesting "natural experiments" in social history. As noted at the beginning of this book, value systems are important in guiding human behavior; these values are placed into people's heads through complex processes of socialization over time; also, these values are subject to change. The interesting natural experiment involves people who are part of the same national value system being placed in drastically different situations for over a generation, plus their consciously and continuously trying to change these values. This is what being placed under a new regime, with new political indoctrination, meant for the East Germans. It is, therefore, hardly surprising that when suddenly reunited, the people of eastern and western Germany felt that some attitudes and outlooks on life were different; they experienced a clash of values, a culture shock.

Some of the early American sociologists, such as William F. Ogburn (1964), realized that values change more slowly than do, for example, the economy and the political system. There is, thus, a condition of **culture lag,** which is not uncommon. Valuable research is now going on that can help us understand much more about the process of socialization and culture lag by measuring exactly how much East and West Germans differ with respect to value orientations. Among others, the research is looking at the following crucial questions: Will eastern and western Germans grow more similar in value orientations? If so, how long will it take? In his speeches before and after the 1998 election, the new chancellor, Gerhard Schroeder, has emphasized that one of his most important goals will be to contribute to the "inner unification" of the two parts of Germany.

Economic Unification

West German social scientist Stephan Eisel provides a good image of what happened in November 1989 to non-Germans trying to understand the situation: "Imagine yourself at home on Christmas day, celebrating with your family, when suddenly you hear a knock at the door. The visitors turn out to be relatives, people with whom you exchange Christmas cards, but otherwise you have not had much contact with them in the last few years" (Eisel 1996:167). These relatives, he goes on to explain, have just lost their home and need help. You are certainly willing and able to help, so invite them to stay with you until things get better. After a few weeks, however, your hospitality runs a bit thin, and your relatives feel guilty about staying, but continue to have nowhere else to go. In essence, this is how East and West Germany were rejoined.

Economic unification between the East and West, as one might understand, has been the most difficult part of unification to achieve and has created the most ill feelings between eastern and western Germany. To begin with, economic conditions in the East were much worse than previously expected: The factories were older, less efficient, and more run down than realized; and there was more redundant labor, fewer resources, and much greater pollution than the former communist government admitted. Second, it had never happened in the history of the world before! Revolutions have changed feudal systems and authoritarian regimes to capitalist democracies and in other places to communist systems. Nowhere had a communist economy been suddenly turned into a capitalist economy. Quite simply, there was extensive disagreement over how it could be done, or even if it could be done.

It is important to realize that how the economic unification was begun by the German government created immense short-term problems. The root of many problems stemmed from the fact that the German government had to act quickly to raise the standard of living of eastern Germans before they all ended up in the West! The German relatives who show up around Christmas time in 1989, in other words, had to be helped quickly and with as little ill feelings as possible.

The first response of the German government, understandably, was to send massive aid to eastern Germany to take care of the growing mass of unemployed and to rebuild the infrastructure of bridges, electricity, telephone service, and so on. In the process, went the reasoning, eastern Germany would also generate new jobs with the infrastructure projects. As of 1997 much had been done: About half the homes in the East have been renovated; and there are many new schools, museums, parks, and shops of all kinds. There are now twice the number of shopping malls per person in the East than in the West. The East also now has 5,000 miles of new highways, 2,800 miles of new railroads, and a phone system among the best in the world—better than that in the West. Further, there have been $600 billion in subsidies to eastern businesses, which helped to bring some $500 billion in new business investments (*New York Times*, April 17, 1997). All of this must be seen as a great achievement and benefit for eastern Germany.

The next problem was what to do with all of the government-owned enterprises, which means virtually all of the previously existing factories in East Germany. To make these factories into more efficient operations, and of course to dismantle the old communist economy, these had to be sold off. A new government agency, the *Treuhand*, was created to do the job. By 1997, about 80 percent of the 16,000 old state-owned factories were privatized, with another 17 percent simply abandoned (Parkes 1997:95; Kocka 1996:198). The enormity of this job, however, cannot be appreciated until one also realizes that in many of the cases of the property sold the courts and the *Treuhand* had to settle disputes of rival ownership, because many of these properties were taken away from Germans when the communist government came into power in the East after World War II.

Now new problems have been added to the old ones: (1) Many redevelopment projects were badly managed and wasteful. For example, $7 billion was devoted to tearing down one old outdated factory and building a new one in its place, creating 2,200 new jobs—at a cost of $3.2 million per job! In other cases, many of the new buildings created some jobs while they were being built, but now stand unused. (2) To pay for this aid and development, the German government went into debt, and the average western citizen had to pay an additional 7.5 percent of their income taxes, as well as higher taxes on such things as gasoline. (3) West German labor laws, higher wages, and more vacation time were quickly exported to the East. Minimum wages were set considerably lower in the East at first, to around $15 per hour, but this was still considerably higher than wages before the fall of the East German government.

These changes at first glance would seem to be positive benefits for eastern Germany, but a first glance is often deceiving. Almost 20 percent of the labor force continues to be unemployed in the East. The problem is that until productivity in the East is considerably improved, a worker being paid $10 to $15 per hour is often unable to create $15 worth of new value in that hour. And on top of this, the eastern part of Germany is surrounded by former communist countries who now have plenty of cheap workers to export or to attract new factory investments for countries like the United States, England, France, and even West German corporations. The eastern Germans with their higher wages are not getting the jobs. In what seems a remarkable turn of events, the Saxony (state) branch of the largest union *(IG Metall)* has been protesting against the higher wages given them by law because they know it is putting them out of work *(International Herald Tribune,* December 11, 1997).

Despite all these problems, and even though the burden with reunification including the relocation of the political institutions to Berlin in 1999 and 2000, will be heavy, there are extensive long-term benefits for both eastern and western Germany because of unification (Hampden-Turner and Trompenaars 1993:199). For example, western Germany has gained a rather well educated and skilled labor force, a large new market, and a back door into the growing markets of the former communist countries of Eastern Europe that are now taking off economically. Also, outsiders must understand that both eastern and western Germans are for the first time in over a generation free to make their own policies, especially for their own long-term benefits. When considering the Nazi terror from the early 1930s, one can say that Germans are really free for the first time in almost 60 years.

As we have already seen, however, Germany at present has considerable economic problems with high unemployment, low economic growth throughout most of the 1990s, and companies that are losing their competitive edge internationally. The burden of German unification outlined above, with many extensive short-term problems and costs, helps explain part of the economic situation Germany finds itself in today. But only part. To fully understand the rest we must turn to changes that the broader world system has undergone since the fall of the old Soviet Union and the Berlin Wall. Before we conclude with this subject and move from Germany to the wider world, however, we need to take one more step beyond Germany and consider the impact and process of European unification.

EUROPEAN UNIFICATION

For many decades, and certainly in the aftermath of World War II, it was the dream of many Europeans to have a unified Europe or some form of European unity. When it gets to the specific means of how such unification will be carried out and how far it may go (few want a United States of Europe, for example), there is disagreement. However, a more unified Europe most likely means a Europe unlikely to go to war again as in World Wars I and II, when millions of Europeans were slaughtered and the continent was divided into hostile camps. Americans often forget that the loss of life, and of course property, was far, far greater for Europeans in those wars than losses for Americans (some 150,000 dead for Americans; tens of millions of Europeans dead). The timing of the European unification is in many ways rather fortunate; a unified Germany is still feared by many of its European neighbors, and thus the coming European unification presents a framework within which the sudden German reunification could take shape in a rather relaxed manner.

It is also interesting to note that in most respects German people have been very supportive of European unification. For years various opinion polls in Europe (often done by the newspaper *The European*) have asked people in various countries about their support for European unification, but with the added dimension of whether the people feel more German (or French, British, Dutch, etc.) or more European. Germans for years have been more in favor of European unification in these polls, and the most likely to say that they feel more European in general than only German. Part of this finding, of course, is related to the tendency for many, especially young Germans, to feel ashamed about the past (also see Winkler 1996:72). But much of the German support for a unified Europe relates to the fact that Germany's neighbors will be more reassured and not fear a unified Germany, and Germany has much to gain economically from European unification. In this section we briefly consider the benefits and changes European unification will bring for Germany. First, we review what the European Union means, elaborating on our introduction to this subject in Chapter 3.

The foundation for what is developing as the European Union today began back in the 1950s with some of the first cooperation between West Germany and France after World War II (Muller 1996:55). This developed into the European Coal and Steel Community to coordinate production in these industries. This was followed by a larger European Economic Community (EEC), later the European Community (EC), and finally in 1993 officially the **European Union** (EU) (Parkes 1997:119). The formation of the European Union occurred with the signing of the **Maastricht Treaty** by the EC leaders in the quaint little Dutch city of Maastricht in 1991. In addition to countries who are already members of the EU, other countries in Europe are being invited to join if they meet economic and political criteria (with respect to such things as government economic policies, budget requirements, democratic institutions, and human rights). The addition of new members will be occurring slowly over the coming years with some of the Eastern European countries freed from Russian domination (e.g., Estonia, Hungary, Poland, Czech Republic, Slovenia).

This, it seems, will be the ultimate test of what the fall of communism in Eastern Europe really means historically, sociologically, and politically: Does the moment of decision for Western capitalist democracies turn into their hegemony in the long run? However, the permanent crisis of the Russian experiment raises the issue whether the Western claim for the universality of its institutions would be invalidated if the spirit of capitalism and the virtue of democracy should prove impossible to transpose to Eastern Europe. Germany, to be sure, is not the only testing ground for what the "triple transition" to capitalism, democracy, and nation-state in this part of the world holds (Offe 1997).

As far as Germany is concerned, there is no question that this transition to unity is much harder to accomplish than Germany's post-war reconstruction. In 1945, most (West) Germans had a similar starting point and an institutional software (market economy, democratic polity and so on) they could work with and wholeheartedly agree on. The first aspect had been lacking in 1989; with the effects of globalization, the drive toward European unification, and its expansion to Eastern Europe, the second aspect, the institutional software that had meant a cultural orientation and individual security to Germans, is in danger of fading away.

As we noted in Chapter 3, the European Union has already allowed the free movement of people to live and work in all member countries (with common passports), promoted the freer movement of services and goods with low or no tariffs, and adopted a common currency, the Euro introduced in 1999, eventually replacing the national currencies (such as the pound, mark, and franc) of the member countries by 2002. But also important, and in many ways more difficult, will be common policies for the member countries with respect to their economies (such as trade and monetary policies), welfare systems, labor regulations, standards on production and health, and pollution restrictions, along with many other areas. To achieve these coordinated policies there is a European Parliament in Strasbourg, France; the European Commission as the governing body in Brussels, Belgium; and the European Central Bank in Frankfurt, Germany. Each nation elects representatives to the European Parliament, which to some extent, controls the work of the commission. The commission, in turn, acts on the orders of the decision-making councils, consisting of the respective ministers of the member nations.

The European Union's Impact on Germany

The leading intent of the EU, of course, is greater economic strength and eventually a united European voice in foreign policy. The EU is also a response to the fear among European countries that North America is being brought together with economic treaties, and that across the Pacific Asia is doing the same (Bornschier 1988, 1994). Together the member states of the EU will have a much larger impact on the world economy, which should help the economies of all members. To the extent that this intent is realized, the German economy will benefit and overcome some of its current problems.

There are also other effects on Germany and the other members that will occur over the years (Thurow 1991:70). Nations with more government spending, higher taxes, higher wages, more welfare benefits, stronger labor unions, extensive labor protection laws, and greater health care benefits, to name just a few, will be pressured to lower these standards. Quite simply, with relatively free movement of people and capital investments within the EU (and around the world), the rich will tend to go to the low-tax countries, corporations will go to the countries with lower wages and weaker labor laws, and the poorer Europeans will tend to migrate to the countries with greater welfare benefits, better health care, and higher wages. Germany, as we have seen, offers more on most of these life quality dimensions than many other European nations, and thus will be pressured to reduce taxes and government spending, wages, labor protection, welfare protection, and health care, as well as their strict pollution and environmental protection.

Behind these problems are value conflicts that we have examined earlier in this book. England, for example, is closer to the United States with its idea of small government, lower taxes, and, simply, less government action in many areas. Germany and France, in particular, are often in opposition to England over these issues. However, England, as well as Germany, France, and the other nations of the EU, will be pressured toward common ground on these issues.

There is another problem: As Bornschier (1995) discovered from interviews conducted around Europe, to a large degree the expansion of the European Union brings into play many conflicting class interests. The corporate elites of Germany, for example, have a strong interest in furthering the EU because it means lower taxes and lower labor costs. The level of protest and even some political violence by workers, the poor, farmers, and the unemployed in some nations of the EU, such as Germany, France, and Belgium that have higher benefits, wages, and protection for the working classes and poor, are likely to increase. Thus, through the end of the 1990s and into the next century, we can expect more political turmoil in Germany as these class conflicts are brought ever more to the forefront of policy changes. France, for example, began 1998 with widespread protests by the unemployed, the poor, and students against low unemployment benefits and welfare payments; 1999 is the time of the farmers who are discontent with the new EU agriculture policy starting in 2000.

THE MODERN WORLD SYSTEM IN CHANGE: THE END OF THE COLD WAR

Lurking behind German reunification and the expanding European Union, however, are even broader changes in the modern world system. Indeed, these broader changes have themselves made both the unification of Germany and the expansion of the EU possible, and in some ways necessary. Unless one steps back to consider these broader changes in the world, the outcome and direction of the changes internal to Europe and Germany cannot be well understood, and responses to them quite likely confused and possibly counterproductive.

We have already considered briefly the basics of the modern world system as described by Wallerstein (1974, 1980, 1989), Chirot (1977, 1986), and others in Chapter 2. To repeat in brief, from about 1500 AD, a new international system based ever more on economic competition was established by northern European nations seeking to recover from the economic stagnation of the 1300s and 1400s. Through worldwide economic expansion they sought to jump-start their economies through the capture of land, resources, and people in less-developed countries around the world. By the beginning of the 20th century most of the less-developed world had been taken by one or another of the dominant European powers. For the newly emerging core nations of Germany, Italy, and Japan, if they were to get their share of land, resources, markets, and people to exploit, it meant taking them from another powerful country. World Wars I and II, as we have seen, were the results.

In the aftermath of World War II, however, the Soviet Union emerged ever stronger, and attempted to defy the basic logic of the modern world system by becoming dominant through military rather than economic might. The capitalist countries, with the United States in the lead, took up the challenge, and as we know, the Soviet Union finally collapsed not long after the Berlin Wall had symbolically and factually fallen down.

Behind this story, however, we must also understand elements of the US economic decline during the 1970s and 1980s. There are clearly many reasons for this relative economic decline of the United States, but two Cold War–related factors were important. First, like the Soviet Union, a greater focus on military spending, rather than the pure logic of capitalist competition, hurt the US economy (Chirot 1986; Kennedy 1987). However, the US economy was much stronger to begin with and could outspend the anticapitalist Soviet economy, leading to the Soviet economic collapse due to the Cold War arms race. The US economy, to be sure, was weakened in the process as well. Second, in international relations during the Cold War, the US made friends and gave favors not so much in its own economic interest, but in the interest of fighting the Soviet Union and its allies in the Cold War. Again, the US economy was harmed to the benefit of US allies.

Even before the collapse of the Soviet Union, the United States reacted to its economic decline with "Reaganomics": a policy of bringing down taxes, reducing government spending and regulations, cutting welfare, and making the rich richer in hope the rich would invest their money properly, make the economy grow, and raise the poor with it. The long-term success of these policies is still in question (Harrison and Bluestone 1988; Reich 1991; Thurow 1991). More likely it was the corporate restructuring, downsizing, and other means of cutting labor costs (such as firing workers, reducing worker benefits, and hiring more temporary workers at lower wages)—in other words, no increase in real income—that led to the American economy roaring back by the middle of the 1990s. While the US economy came roaring back, however, so did high levels of economic inequalities and all of the social problems that can result (Kerbo 1996).

In tandem with these changes came revisions in US foreign policy: No longer would European and Japanese economic protectionism be accepted by the United States simply because they were allies in the fight against communism. And no longer could US trade and investment be assured because of a nation's strong anticommunist stand. American trade and investment began moving, in general, more to Asia, and throughout the Americas, which increasingly made the Europeans nervous.

The Japanese, but particularly the Europeans, have certainly taken notice of signs the US economy may be becoming more competitive in relation to their own, and how American corporations have been making it possible. England had been following the US lead with some economic improvement since the first years of Reaganomics. For Europe in general, however, the focus on economic unification had been the major objective to improve economic competitiveness (Bornschier 1995, 1994). With far higher taxes, welfare and unemployment benefits, more generous pay and benefits to workers, and much shorter working hours than the United States, many Europeans are now becoming worried that they will be left behind if the new conservative, pro-business American strategy succeeds in making the US economy much more competitive again. European leaders, such as Germany's previous chancellor, Kohl, and his successor, Gerhard Schroeder, have been making speeches to this effect, with some small government policy changes to go along with the new talk. Some of the measures taken by Kohl's government to reduce welfare spending and the influence of labor in major German corporations were rejected by most Germans, in part resulting in his party losing the national elections in September 1998 and a new Social Democratic–Green Party coalition coming into power to reverse some of these changes. Germany is thus faced with a difficult dilema: Most of the German population rejects the high inequality and low welfare costs that may in part be responsible for the strong US economy, but, of course, they also reject the high unemployment and less competitive economy that Germany currently finds itself with. The central political issue as the new government took office in October 1998 was how to keep the more humane economy favored by most Germans and at the same time make the economy more competitive in the new world economy.

CONCLUSION

Whether or not the American model (that is, the renewed stress on cutting wages and benefits, while increasing working hours for those with jobs) will in fact help regain and maintain US economic dominance in the long run, however, is far from certain. A growing, though still limited, number of scholars and economists in the United States have been arguing that America can only regain economic strength, not to mention develop a society with fewer social problems, by moving in the opposite direction (see especially Thurow 1991; Reich 1991). In a similar manner, others have argued that the United States should look closely at how Germany is able to train its workforce and obtain more worker involvement in corporate decision making as a way to improve competitiveness and to keep social peace (Thelen 1991; Turner 1991; Wever 1991).

The argument, in short, is that America needs a better educated, better trained, better paid, and more motivated and loyal workforce in a world economy that increasingly rewards regions able to compete in high-tech industries. As Thurow (1991) put it, America must compete in a new world economy of high tech by worrying more about the education and motivation of the bottom 50 percent of workers and families, rather than beating down wages and labor as has been done in the past. In the view of many, it is the better educated, more skilled, and more loyal workers (because of more labor participation and union involvement) of Europe and Japan that will give those countries the edge in future economic competition if the United States does not make changes in these directions.

The modern world system is set for the next stage of core competition in the 21st century. Will the 21st century belong to a resurgent America with its new policies of cutting wages and benefits, thus increasing inequality, while continuing to invest less in education and social welfare for families and children? Or, will the better educated and better paid labor of Europe and Japan, with more long-term commitment and loyalty to companies, make more gains and cause more relative economic decline for the United States through the 21st century?

The stakes are high, and the policies that finally emerge as creating the stronger economic performer will determine the shape of the future societies of Germany and the United States, as well as the rest of the world. What is certain, however, is that the Europe of the 21st century will no longer be the Atlantic Europe of the Cold War but rather the new Continental Europe under German hegemony. Germany's reunification, its dominance in terms of economic potential and population size, and its geopolitical position between Eastern and Western Europe testify to this change. Further testimony is given by a political commentator who said that Germany took over the leading role in Europe from the old Soviet Union, the former's deutsche mark replacing Russia's soldiers (Nenning 1990).

END NOTES

1. Right-wing radicals were successful in their agitation against the treaty as the "dictate of Versailles," although its conditions were not as tough as, for example, Germany had imposed upon France after the defeat of 1871 or upon Russia in the Peace of Brest-Litowsk in 1917. In fact, Great Britain and France waived some of the reparations in exchange for forcing the German delegation to sign the so-called Article 231, which depicted Germany as the sole initiator of the "great war" and all the damages that had gone with it. By declaring Germany to have been defeated and guilty, the right-wing radicals could easily speed the "stab-in-the-back legend" (*Dolchstosslegende*) and thus accuse the Social Democratic government with its president, Friedrich Ebert, of having betrayed an army that was "undefeated in the field." This kind of propaganda soon escalated into smaller rebellions, one of which was the "Kapp-Putsch" of 1920 in which the army refused to support the government. There were also a number of killings with the leftist Rosa Luxemburg and Karl Liebknecht as victims in 1919.

2. Compared to other European nations, the Federal Republic may be located between two types of organizing politics: the consensus-oriented democracy of Austria in which political power shared by the major parties in "great" coalitions pervades almost all walks of life, on the one hand, and the more competitive democracy of Great Britain, scorned by Lord Hailsham as "elective dictatorship," on the other. That is to say, in Germany you find both (mostly "small") coalitions and political interlocking as well as hard competition between political parties (see Ismayr 1997). Germany's proportional electoral system gives even small parties a chance not only to gain votes and seats in the parliament but also to be an indispensable coalition partner on both the federal and the state level (e.g., the FDP and now the Green Party).

3. Unquestionably, former chancellor Helmut Kohl whose Christian Democrats had formed the government in a coalition with the Free Democrats since 1982, was highly respected by other heads of states, including Ronald Reagan, George Bush, and Bill Clinton, for his political farsightedness and his contribution to the German reunification and the European integration process. Some observers, like the French philosopher André Glucksmann, see Kohl as "the greatest Chancellor of the Germans" (*Die Welt*, October 1, 1998). While Bismarck had created the Reich as a union of German dukes "from above," Kohl effectively channeled the decisive impulses toward unification "from below."

    However, after 16 years of Chancellor Kohl many Germans seem to have opted for a change as Kohl's government was not able to pass much-needed laws (e.g., the tax reform) or effectively bring down the high unemployment rate. Some Germans seem to have trusted more his opponent, the young and eloquent Social Democrat Schroeder, to master the challenges of the near future, while others simply hoped a change in faces would also bring a change in politics.

4. Baden-Württemberg, Bayern, Berlin, Bremen, Hamburg, Hessen, Niedersachsen, Nordrhein-Westfalen, Rheinland-Pfalz, Saarland, and Schleswig-Holstein are the 11 "old states" and Brandenburg, Mecklenburg-Vorpommern, Sachsen, Sachsen-Anhalt and Thüringen are the 5 "new states".

5. It is true that American banks manage a large percentage of corporate stock from US corporations. However, the American banks do not own this stock, but manage it for pension funds and trust funds. The German banks, in contrast, own this corporate stock. American banks have some influence over these corporations, but far short of the influence German banks have over other corporations (Kerbo 1996).

6. Early German sociologists, such as Georg Simmel (1905, 1955), outlined similar principles of human societies in dealing with conflicting interests. These sociologists have shown how group conflicts, when properly managed and organized, can in fact have positive benefits for both parties in a conflict (Coser 1956, 1967). For example, it has long been pointed out that an organized opponent is much preferable to an unorganized one. With an unorganized opponent, solutions to a conflict or compromise are close to impossible. But with an organized opponent, negotiations and compromises can be reached. And, most importantly, the compromise agreement can be carried out with an organized opponent whose leaders are able to keep their members in line. Recent studies of German executive attitudes toward strong unions and works councils suggest that most have read their Simmel. As one representative of the Associations of German Employers stated:

> As soon as you get splinter groups in the plant, you get unrest in the plant as well. We would rather deal with one union, with a unified works council. A single, unified opponent is more reliable and trustworthy [verlaesslich]; more than one faction fosters competition among them as each tries to outdo the other. We would rather have a single strong and self-confident union to work with (Thelen 1991:34–35).

7. We should note that this does not necessarily mean that the top 20 percent of the population became poorer. The figures on income refer to the "income pie" and how it is shared. If the income pie has grown, as it certainly did in this time period, the top 20 percent were indeed richer, but more of the increase in the income pie went to less affluent groups compared to before. What is actually more important than these changes in relative inequalities is the change in absolute terms in that most Germans are better off in the 1980s than in the 1950s. This is what sociologists call the *elevator effect*: All move up a story or two but the distances remain by and large the same (Beck 1992).

8. Data are from government sources compiled by the U.S. Senate Subcommittee on Oversight of Government Management in 1991. See the *Los Angeles Times,* Feb. 7, 1992.

9. To make the point more clearly we can provide a few details pertaining to the influence of works councils from the 239-page 1991 English version of the official Codetermination Laws (German Federal Ministry of Labor and Social Affairs 1991:18–19):

[Works councils have] a genuine right of codetermination in a series of matters such as: working hours, e.g. the introduction of short-time work, the introduction and use of technical devices designed to monitor the behavior or performance of the employees, the assignment of and notice to vacate company-owned accommodation, the fixing of job and bonus rates and comparable performance-related remuneration.

Works councils have a far-reaching right of participation and co-determination in matters concerning the structuring, organization and design of jobs, operation and the working environment, manpower planning and personnel management as well as in-plant training.

In the case of recruitments, gradings, re-gradings and transfers the employer must obtain the consent of the works council. If the works council refuses its consent it can be substituted only by a decision in lieu of consent by a labor court.

Dismissals are effective only if the works council was consulted in advance. The works council may oppose a routine dismissal with the effect that the employer must keep the employee in his employment until a final court decision is given on the case at issue.

The works council has the right to be informed on a large number of matters. Moreover, the finance committee, which is to be established in companies with more than 100 employees, and whose members are all appointed by the works council, has a substantial right to be informed and to be heard in financial matters.

In the case of alterations, such as the reduction of operations, the closure or transfer of an establishment, the works council may require the preparation of a social compensation plan in order to compensate for any financial prejudices sustained by the employees.

10. Much of the information about wealthy capitalist families in Germany today and before World War II has been kindly supplied by Professors Leonard Broom and William L. Shay from their ongoing research on wealthy capitalist families in Germany (Broom and Shay 1992).

11. The recent restrictions of the German asylum law may serve as a case in point. As a consequence, many refugees had been denied entrance into Germany or had been sent home again, although, as many social scientists on the left and church communities believed, the refugees involved were in danger of losing life or freedom upon return. In some cases, the church communities granted them "church asylum," since the state, according to an unwritten law, does not enter churches by force. In the meantime, the church community would try to convince the state authority to reexamine these cases. There are other developments, such as the increase of porno-graphic and violent TV programs, of distance between people and of right-wing radicalism that churches have criticized and exposed publicly.

12. In an article entitled "Die Deutschen auf dem Weg in die heidnische Gesellschaft" (The Germans on the way into a godless society), the widely read news magazine *Der Spiegel* (No. 52, December 22, 1997) speaks of 67 percent. In the former GDR, 46 percent of the population belonged to the

Protestant Church, only 7 percent were Catholics, and 45 percent had no religious affiliation. Today, religious belief is very important only to 13 percent of the Germans in the West and 7 percent in the East, while for 52 percent (79 percent in the East) it is either less important or without any meaning (Glunk 1996:319).

13. In a survey taken in 1992, 68 percent of those who left the Catholic Church indicated as their main reason Rome's position on contraception and divorce; 59 percent said they left because they did not want to pay church tax; and 49 percent said the church's opinion on actual problems was decisive (Glunk 1996:319).

14. The numbers of Muslim people in Germany given by such expert authors as Bassam Tibi (1996) and Muhammed S. Abdullan (1993) vary quite a bit. Tibi talks about an Islamic minority, the "diaspora Islam in Europe" with 2 million members, while Abdullah refers to 3 million Muslims. Other authors such as Yasemin Karakasoglu allege 2.5 million Muslims in Germany in the mid-1990s.

15. The German weekly newspaper *Das Parlament* (July 7, 1997) reported under the title "Die Bundesrepublik Deutschland ist ein Einwanderungsland geworden" (The Federal Republic has become an immigration country) extensively about the churches' statement on the "foreigner law" (see also Strasser 1997a).

16. During 1998 a new study of poverty was released suggesting that the rate of German children living in poverty had increased to just over 10 percent (*International Herald Tribune*, August 26, 1998). As is often the case, however, when comparing such information across societies, one must be careful with definitions. The measure of poverty used in this study was whether or not the children lived in households defined as poor enough to receive welfare benefits. Thus, this measure of poverty is considerably higher than what is used in the United States, and these German children even receive welfare benefits that move them out of poverty. The 20 percent of children living in poverty in the United States are defined as living in poverty *after* including income from their parents' welfare, which unlike Germany seldom brings them even above the much lower definition of poverty in the United States.

17. However, a study by the Institute of Labor Market and Occupational Research of the official Federal Board of Labor shows that 61 percent of the long-term unemployed can only be employed as "unqualified workers" and 40 percent have health problems. 42 percent of the long-term unemployed, that is, almost half of them, have never or for a long time not worked before registering as unemployed (Unternehmerverband Ruhr Niederrhein e.V. 1998:60).

18. A description of this was given to us during interviews with Japanese business executives living in the Düsseldorf area in the early 1990s. One Japanese man told us how a group of young men appearing to be neo-Nazis started to attack him one night, but after they learned he was Japanese, they apologized and left (Kerbo, Wittenhagen, and Nakao 1994a and b). It seemed that the neo-Nazis had at first taken him for one of the 60,000 poor Vietnamese guest workers who were initially admitted by the East German government and who are now slowly being repatriated and are

blamed for taking jobs away from Germans. This motivation is of course closely linked with economic tides, as recent state elections in the Eastern part of Germany with substantial gains of the right-wing party DVU demonstrate. Of course, this may be protest or, to return to some of the ideas expressed at the beginning of this book, an expression of the socialized longing for being told what is good and how one should go about realizing it.

19. The American author of this book once brought surprise and puzzled smiles to a group of German students when referring to one who had a German father and a Mexican mother as *Mexican-German*. Such terminology doesn't exist in Germany as in the United States with terms such as Asian-Americans and African-Americans. To top it off, the non-American author of this book is not German either: He is Austrian, although a lifetime German civil servant who was offered German citizenship immediately after his appointment to the chair at the University of Duisburg. His wife, by the way, is German, his daughter has three passports (American because of birth in the United States, Austrian because of her father, and German because of her mother) and his son two (Austrian and German).

20. Upon closer inspection this argument, as especially used by the former German government, does not really hold water. Germany has witnessed several "labor migrations." The first occurring in the 18th century under the Prussian King Frederick the Great who welcomed the Protestant Huguenots from Catholic France, mostly well-educated and generally well-to-do people; the second starting in the second half of the 19th century with the industrialization of the Ruhr area that attracted mainly people from the east, as the many Polish names in Duisburg, Essen, and Dortmund still prove today; and the third migration to Germany taking place under the auspices of the post–World War II economic miracle, which attracted many labor migrants from southern Europe but especially from Turkey, at first almost only males, later also their families. In the 20th century at least, Germany has been known as a country of emigrants rather than of immigrants, and Germany has never seen itself as a country of immigration but rather as one of "guest workers." Every time, however, workers were called and humans came. Sometimes one is reminded of the old Greek concept of the guest as one who leaves again and is therefore treated with hospitality while the barbarian stays and hence can be killed (see Strasser 1997a).

GLOSSARY

bank keiretsu   In Japan, a *keiretsu* refers to groups of private companies with informal ties and agreements of cooperation at the top of the Japanese business world. In Germany, a *bank keiretsu* refers to a similar system but with the central member being a large bank that owns much stock in other corporations and, thus, has significant control over these other corporations.

Basic Law   Germany's Federal Constitution adopted after World War II, which has now been extended to the unified Germany in 1990.

Bundesrat   A kind of upper house of the current German parliamentary system by means of which the states *(Laender)* of the Federal Republic, presently 16, participate in the legislative process of the Federal Republic. Its members are bound by the orders of the states.

Bundestag   The more powerful lower house of the current German parliamentary system made up of representatives directly elected by the German people. As a body, the Bundestag elects and can vote out of office the federal chancellor (much like a prime minister), elects half of the members of the Federal Constitutional Court, and constitutes half of the members of the Federal Assembly *(Bundesversammlung)*, which elects the federal president. The Bundestag, as the highest legislative organ, ratifies international treaties, decides on the budget, and is in charge of national defense policies and action. It controls the federal government and its administration.

capitalist development state   A capitalist economy wherein the state has extensive control in managing the economy with major policies oriented toward economic development and industrialization.

capitalist system   An economic system in which the means of production (factories, machines, banks, and so on) are for the most part privately owned and operated for private profit.

chancellor   The leader of the German federal government, much like a prime minister, elected by members of the German Bundestag and vested with the so-called guideline competence.

class   In one of the most general definitions, it is a grouping of individuals with similar positions of power and similar political and economic interests within the stratification system. According to Max Weber, it is a dimension of social stratification based upon property ownership or the lack of ownership (as in Marxist theory) but also on occupational skills, educational qualifications, and income.

codetermination   The Codetermination Law of 1976 grants employees the right to participate in decision-making bodies if their economic, social, and personal interests are affected. The Codetermination Law allows for worker influence on three levels: (1) decisions affecting the entire economy or industries can be influenced by the unions; (2) decisions within particular companies are influenced by elected works councils on the shop floor as described by the Works Constitution Act; and (3) participation in decisions on corporate policies in the steel and coal mining industries as well as in corporations with more than 2,000 employees through the requirement that half of the members of their boards of trustees (boards of directors) be elected from employees of the corporation.

collectivistic value system   A value system that stresses the group is more important than the individual and individual desires. It assumes that the whole is more than the sum of its parts and, hence, requires greater sacrifice for group interests.

crude birth rate   The number of births in a given year per 1,000 people in the society.

culture   Most broadly defined as the learned part of human behavior. Anthropologists have, therefore, defined it as the total way of life of a people. Culture is the blueprint for living, including rules for behavior called *norms* as well as broader belief systems, called *values.*

culture lag   A conflict between the more rapidly changing technology or material conditions in a society and the more slowly changing nonmaterial culture. For example, the possibilities of the Internet change much more rapidly than the laws regulating its uses can be passed.

demography   The study of population characteristics and their changes.

dual system   The combination of labor representation by unions and legally mandated works councils in postwar Germany. A second meaning refers to the German idea of apprenticeship that combines secondary schooling (*Berufsschule*) with on-the-job training.

ethnic group   A group of people relatively distinct in cultural background, especially when they come from another society with a different language, religion, and racial origin, compared to the dominant group in the society.

ethnic minorities   A group of people in a subordinate position with respect to economic opportunities and political power in the society with a relatively distinct cultural background compared with the dominant group in the society (e.g., Mexican-Americans in the United States, Turks in Germany).

ethnocentrism   The assumption that the beliefs and practices of people from another society and culture are inferior to the beliefs and practices of one's own society and culture, which are held to be "correct" and superior.

European Union (EU)   Following the European Economic Community (EEC) in 1957 and the European Community (EC) in 1967, the union of European nations was officially established in 1993 based upon the Maastricht Treaty signed in 1991. The member nations of the EU have a parliament located in Strasbourg, France, with representatives elected by the people of the member states. The parliament thus far has only little legislative power and control over the executive branch, the European Commission in Brussels.

extended families   A family grouping that consists of more than two generations with authority vested in the oldest members.

fascist   A political movement and ideology based upon totalitarian political rule favoring the upper classes in society; usually combined with strong racist, nationalistic, antisocialist, or anticommunist beliefs. Today's right-wing movement is called neofascist.

federal president   The symbolic head of the Federal Republic of Germany who is elected by the Federal Assembly (*Bundesversammlung*).

Federal Republic of Germany   The official name of the German state and government today.

federal system   A system of national government that recognizes and gives some independent authority to regional governing bodies such as states in the United States or *Laender* in the current German system of government.

fertility rate   The number of births per 1,000 women of child-bearing age in a society.

feudalism   An agrarian system of social stratification based upon land ownership with a high level of ascription.

forced industrialization   A method of industrialization in which the state forces heavy investment in basic industries, with low wages to workers and peasants so that all surplus profits can be reinvested for more economic development.

German Democratic Republic (GDR)   The official name of the East German communist government, which was established in the Soviet occupation zone after World War II and fell after the collapse of the Berlin Wall in 1989.

government ministry   Divisions of the executive branch of government such as a Foreign Ministry, or Finance Ministry, which in European nations have more independent power to govern affairs when compared to departments of the executive branch in the United States.

Holocaust   The systematic attempt at genocide of the Jewish people and other people disliked by the Nazi Party in Germany during its reign (1933–1945), which resulted in the murder of at least six million Jews.

individualistic value system   A value system stressing the greater importance of the individual and individual freedoms over group's needs and collective restraints.

institutions   Sets of values, roles, and obligations centered around important tasks that must be fulfilled within a society. The family, economy, education, religion, polity (the way formal power is organized), and the criminal justice system are all examples of institutions within modern societies.

judicial branch   The branch of government charged with maintaining the legal system and interpreting the laws of government.

Junker   The feudal class of landed aristocracy in Germany, especially in its eastern parts.

Laender   Official divisions on a regional level within the German federal system of government similar to individual states in the United States.

Maastricht Treaty   The treaty signed in the Dutch town of Maastricht in 1991 that created the European Union in 1993.

Marshall Plan   The European Recovery Program (ERP) in the years following its enactment by the U.S. Congress on April 3, 1948, that provided massive loans and other forms of economic support, including food, to West Germany and other allied nations, which helped bring about rapid economic recovery. It was named after George C. Marshall, then Secretary of State.

modern world system   The system of unequal power and economic roles among nations similar to an international stratification system, which has been closely linked with the development of capitalism and colonialism since the 1500s.

multidimensional view of social stratification   The perspective originated by Max Weber that argues that Marx's view of ownership versus nonownership of the means of production as the most important dimension of social stratification is too simple. Rather, Weber stressed that class, status, and power (or party) can be important dimensions of structured social inequality.

National Socialist Party of Germany   The official name of Hitler's Nazi Party (*NSDAP* for *Nationalsozialistische Deutsche Arbeiterpartei*).

NATO   (North Atlantic Treaty Organization) The military treaty established after World War II that united the Western Allies opposed to the Soviet Union and the Warsaw Pact in a common military defense system. NATO is today being extended to Eastern European nations and planned as a common military defense organization for Europe. Its headquarters is in Brussels, Belgium.

nuclear family   A family system that includes only the married couple and their children as the main family unit within the society.

parliamentary system   A democratic system of government in which representatives are elected by the people. Once elected, they are in charge of forming a government that elects the head of government, a prime minister or a chancellor in the case of Germany, from within the members of parliament.

patriarchical   A family system that gives more power to the male members within the family, and usually traces the family line through the male's side of the family (patrilineal system).

political violence   Violence used in attempts to bring about or resist political change, usually occurring in revolutions, riots, and civil wars.

power   The dimension of stratification which, according to Max Weber, is based upon differential authority as a means to influence others in society. Weber referred especially to bureaucratic organizations such as states and economic corporations in need of power vested in positions to realize goals.

racism   A belief system defining groups of people as either superior or inferior on the basis of biological characteristics.

Reichstag   The parliament of Germany between 1871 and 1945; also the name of the building in Berlin, finished in 1894, that housed the Reichstag until 1933 when it was burned down (by the Dutch communist Marinus van der Lubbe, enabling the Nazis to legalize the persecution of political enemies) and the home of the Bundestag again after the government and representatives moved from Bonn to Berlin in 1999.

revolutions   Organized attempts to bring about fundamental change in society and the government using political violence and directed toward the overthrow of the ruling classes in the society.

sect   A relatively small religious organization that either deviates from, or actually opposes, the teachings of mainstream religions, but which, unlike cults, is not normally secretive or seen as completely illegitimate by the majority of people in the society (e.g., Jehovah's Witnesses, Scientology Church in Germany).

social mobility   Movement to a significant degree up or down within a system of social stratification. Social mobility is often divided into two types: intergenerational social mobility, movement up or down compared to one's parents; and intragenerational social mobility, movement up or down in one's own lifetime or career.

social movements   Purposeful organized attempts by individuals and groups to produce social change within a society through reforms or revolutions (e.g., women's movement, labor movement, neighborhood initiatives). As soon as social movements become bureaucratic organizations such as political parties, they give up their basic characteristic of existence, to pursue their cause voluntarily.

social stratification   The condition in which a hierarchy of social layers based on an inequality of social resources (e.g., income, prestige, qualification) has been hardened or institutionalized, and there is a system of social relationships that determines and more or less reproduces who gets what and why.

social structure   A system of social relationships among individuals within groups and among groups or categories of people in society. This is the network of social relations that are the building blocks of societies and based upon processes of social differentiation (e.g., age, sex, region) and social hierarchization (e.g., income, prestige, power) as well as a combination of them (e.g., classes, strata).

status   Ranking based upon honor or prestige within society. According to Max Weber, the dimension of social stratification based upon respect and following a specifically honored life style in the society.

status attainment   The process whereby individuals reach a given status-position. Status can be attained on the basis of achievement or ascriptive factors or a mixture of both. It determines where people end up in the class system. Status attainment research is an important branch of the study of social stratification.

upper class   Old, established families with significant ownership of major corporations or land and therefore extensive influence, economic power, and, hence, status flowing from such ownership, often expressed in a specific lifestyle tradition.

value orientations   Broad preferences for ideals and beliefs within a society's culture, such as individualism, that shape more specific beliefs, practices, norms, and laws within the society.

Weimar Republic   The period of liberal democratic government in Germany (1919–33), named after the city of Weimar in which the constitutional assembly met in 1919. Its collapse was due to the economic hardships during the late 1920s and the early 1930s, the permanent conflicts between political parties, and the discontent of major groups (especially the old and new elites) with the new form of government and with economic development.

works council   The board of worker representatives (*Betriebsrat*) elected by employees in German companies and government agencies, defined by the Works Constitution Act and Codetermination Law, that gives the worker representatives considerable influence on many aspects of the workplace, including employing and dismissing personnel.

REFERENCES

Abdullah, Muhammed S. 1993. *Was will der Islam in Deutschland?* Gütersloh: Gütersloher Verlagshaus.

Abegglen, James C., and George Stalk, Jr. 1985. *Kaisha: The Japanese Corporation.* New York: Basic Books.

Anweiler, Oskar, Hans-Jurgen Fuchs, Martina Daner, and Eberhard Petermann, eds. 1992. *Bildungspolitik in Deutschland 1945–1990.* Bonn: Bundeszentrale für politische Bildung.

Ardagh, John. 1987. *Germany and the Germans: An Anatomy of Society Today.* New York: Harper & Row.

Backes, Uwe. 1997. "Rechtsextremismus in Deutschland. Ideologien, Organisationen und Strategien." *Aus Politik und Zeitgeschichte* 9–10:27–35.

Bärsch, Claus-Ekkehard. 1998. *Die politische Religion des Nationalsozialismus.* Munich: Fink.

Barz, Heiner. 1994. "Jugend und Religion in den neuen Bundesländern." *Aus Politik und Zeitgeschichte* 38:21–31.

Beck, Ulrich. 1992. *Risk Society: Towards a New Modernity.* London: Sage.

Beine, Jürgen. 1995. "Tabellen und Graphiken zur Wirtschafts- und Gesellschaftsgeschichte Nordrhein-Westfalens 1815–1995." In *Gesellschafts- und Wirtschaftsgeschichte Rheinlands und Westfalens,* ed. D. Briesen et al., 269–91. Stuttgart: Kohlhammer.

Bellers, Juergen, and Anni Bellers. 1997. *Die DDR tickt weiter: Wie die Ostdeutschen denken.* Muenster: LIT-Verlag.

Bendix, Reinhard. 1978. *Kings or People: Power and the Mandate to Rule.* Berkeley: University of California Press.

Bendix, Reinhard, and Seymour Martin Lipset, eds. 1966. *Class, Status and Power: Social Stratification in Comparative Perspective.* 2nd ed. New York: Free Press.

Bertram, Hans. 1997. *Kinder in nichtehelichen Lebensgemeinschaften.* Opladen: Leske & Budrich.

Blau, Judith, and Peter Blau. 1982. "The Cost of Inequality: Metropolitan Structure and Violent Crime." *American Sociological Review* 47:114–29.

Blossfeld, Hans-Peter. 1985. *Bildungsexpansion und Berufschancen: Empirische Analysen zur Lage der Berufsanfänger.* Frankfurt/M.: Campus.

———. 1987. "Entry into the Labor Market and Occupational Career in the Federal Republic." In *Comparative Studies of Social Structure: Recent Research on France, the United States, and the Federal Republic of Germany,* ed. Wolfgang Teckenberg, 86–118. Armonk, NY: M. E. Sharpe.

Bornschier, Volker. 1988. *Westliche Gesellschaft im Wandel.* Frankfurt: Campus.

———. 1994. "The Rise of the European Community: Grasping Toward Hegemony? or Therapy Against National Decline?" *International Journal of Sociology* 24:62–96.

———. 1995. *Western Society in Transition*. New Bruswick, NJ: Transaction Press.

Bourdieu, Pierre. 1984. *Distinction: A Social Critique of the Judgment of Taste*. London: Routledge.

Broom, Leonard, and William L. Shay, Jr. 1992."German Billionaires and the Fortunes of War." Unpublished working paper.

Brunt, P.A. 1971. *Social Conflicts in the Roman Republic*. London: Chatto and Windus.

Buerklin, Wilhelm, Heike Rebenstorf, et al. 1997. *Eliten in Deutschland: Rekrutierung und Integration*. Opladen: Leske+Budrich.

Burgess, Ernest W. 1925. "The Growth of the City." In *The City*, eds. Robert E. Park and Ernest W. Burgess, 47–62. Chicago: University of Chicago Press.

Burkart, G. 1995. "Zum Strukturwandel der Familie—Mythen und Fakten." *Aus Politik und Zeitgeschichte* 52–53:3–13.

Carroll, Glenn R., and Karl Ulrich Mayer. 1986. "Job-Shift Patterns in the Federal Republic of Germany: The Effects of Social Class, Industrial Sector and Organizational Size." *American Sociological Review* 51:323–42.

Chirot, Daniel. 1977. *Social Change in the Twentieth Century*. New York: Harcourt Brace Jovanovich.

———. 1978. "Social Change in Communist Romania." *Social Forces,* 57:457–99.

———. 1984. "The Rise of the West." *American Sociological Review* 50:181–195.

———. 1986. *Social Change in the Modern Era*. New York: Harcourt Brace Jovanovich.

Clark, Kenneth. 1969. *Civilization*. New York: Harper & Row.

Collins, Randall. 1975. *Conflict Sociology*. New York: Academic Press.

Coser, Lewis. 1956. *The Functions of Social Conflict*. New York: Free Press.

———. 1967. *Continuities in the Study of Social Conflict*. New York: Free Press.

Craig, Gordon A. 1991. *The Germans*. New York: Meridian.

Dahrendorf, Ralf. 1965a. *Arbeiterkinder an deutschen Universitäten*. Tübingen: Mohr.

———. 1965b. *Bildung ist Bürgerrecht. Plädoyer für eine aktive Bildungspolitik*. Hamburg: Wegner.

———. 1979. *Society and Democracy in Germany*. NewYork: Norton.

Davies, Norman. 1996. *Europe: A History*. New York: Oxford University Press.

Davis, Nancy J., and Robert V. Robinson. 1991. "Men's and Women's Consciousness of Gender Inequality: Austria, West Germany, Great Britain, and the United States." *American Sociological Review* 56:72–84.

de Tocqueville, Alexis. 1969. *Democracy in America*. New York: Doubleday.

Dettling, Warnfried. 1986. "Krise des Wohlfahrtsstaates." In *Soziale Ungleichheit und Sozialpolitik: Legitimation, Wirkung, Programmatik*. eds. Jürgen Krüger and Hermann Strasser. 193–99. Regensburg: Transfer Verlag.

Dicke, Klaus. 1993. "Ausländer." In *Handbuch zur deutschen Einheit*, ed. Werner Weidenfeld and Karl-Rudolf Korte, 19–25. Bonn: Bundeszentrale für politische Bildung.

Dietrich, William S. 1991. *In The Shadow of the Rising Sun: The Political Roots of American Economic Decline*. University Park, PA: Pennsylvania State University Press.

Domhoff, G. William. 1998. *Who Rules America, Power and Politics in 2000.* Mountain View, CA: Mayfield.

———. 1983. *Who Rules America Now?: A View for the '80s.* Englewood Cliffs, NJ: Prentice Hall.

Dorbritz, J., and K. Gärtner. 1995. "Bericht 1995 über die demographische Lage in Deutschland." *Zeitschrift für Bevölkerungswissenschaft* 20:339–448.

Drauschke, Petra, and Margit Stolzenberg. 1995. "Familie." In *Sozialreport 1995. Daten und Fakten zur sozialen Lage in den neuen Bundesländern,* 276–328. Berlin: Hans-Böckler-Stiftung.

Durkheim, Emile. 1948. *The Elementary Forms of the Religious Life.* Glencoe, IL.: Free Press.

Eisel, Stephan. 1996. "Political Dynamics in Germany." In *In Search of Germany,* eds. Michael Mertes, Steven Muller, and Heinrich August Winkler, 167–90. New Brunswick, NJ: Transaction Books.

EKD (Evangelische Kirche in Deutschland, Kirchenamt). 1998a. Statistische Beilage zum Amtsblatt der EKD, No. 92, H.11. Hanover: EKD.

———. 1998b. Das gottesdienstliche Leben in der evangelischen Kirche (Flyer October 1998). Hanover: EKD.

Erbsloeh, Barbara, Thomas Hagelstange, Dieter Holtmann, Joachim Singelmann, and Hermann Strasser. 1990. *Ende der Klassengesellschaft?* Regensburg: Transfer Verlag.

Erikson, Robert, and John H. Goldthorpe. 1992. *The Constant Flux: A Study of Class Mobility in Industrial Societies.* Oxford: Clarendon.

Europäische Kommission, ed. 1996. *Die demographische Lage in der Europäischen Union 1995.* Brussels: European Commission.

European Commission. 1997. *Beschäftigung in Europa 1997.* Luxembourg: Amt für amtliche Veröffentlichungen der Europäischen Gemeinschaften.

Falke, Andreas. 1990. "Regional und Stadtentwicklung." In *Länderbericht U.S.A. Vol. II: Gesellschaft, Aussenpolitik, Kultur, Religion, Erziehung,* eds. W.P. Adams et al., 183–205. Frankfurt/M.: Campus.

Fallows, James. 1994. *Looking at the Sun: The Rise of the New East Asian Economic and Political System.* New York: Pantheon.

Featherman, David, and Robert Hauser. 1978. *Opportunity and Change.* New York: Academic Press.

Fischer, Andreas. 1992. *Das Bildungssystem der DDR. Entwicklung, Umbruch und Neugestaltung seit 1989.* Darmstadt: Wiss. Buchgesellschaft.

Fischer, Bernd-Reiner. 1994. "Bildung." In *Handbuch zur deutschen Einheit,* ed. Werner Weidenfeld and Karl-Rudolf Korte, 55–63. Bonn: Bundeszentrale für politische Bildung.

Flaig, Berthold Bodo, Thomas Meyer, and Jörg Ueltzhöffer. 1994. *Alltagsästhetik und politische kultur.* 2nd ed. Bonn: Dietz.

Flamini, Roland. 1997. *Passport Germany.* San Rafael, CA: World Trade Press.

Fuerstenberg, Friedrich. 1995. "Deutschlands Wirtschaft nach der Wende." In *Deutschland nach der Wende. Eine Zwischenbilanz,* ed. Robert Hettlage and Karl Lenz, 93–118. Munich: Beck.

Garten, Jeffrey E. 1992. *A Cold Peace: America, Japan, Germany, and the Struggle for Supremacy.* New York: Times Books.

Geiger, Theodor. 1932. *Die soziale Schichtung des deutschen Volkes.* Stuttgart: Enke.

Geissler, Rainer. 1995a. "Das gefährliche Gerücht von der hohen Ausländerkriminalität." *Aus Politik und Zeitgeschichte* 35: 30–39.

———. 1995b. "Neue Strukturen der sozialen Ungleichheit im vereinten Deutschland." In *Deutschland nach der Wende. Eine Zwischenbilanz,* eds. Robert Hettlage and Karl Lenz, 119–41. Munich: Beck.

———. 1996. *Die Sozialstruktur Deutschlands. Zur gesellschaftlichen Entwicklung mit einer Zwischenbilanz zur Vereinigung.* 2nd ed. Opladen: Westdeutscher Verlag.

———. ed. 1994. *Soziale Schichtung und Lebenschancen in Deutschland.* 2nd ed. Stuttgart: Enke.

Gerlach, Michael L. 1992. *Alliance Capitalism: The Social Organization of Japanese Business.* Berkeley: University of California Press.

German Federal Ministry of Labor and Social Affairs. 1991. *Codetermination in the Federal Republic of Germany (Legal Texts).* Bonn: Der Bundesminister für Arbeit und Sozialordnung.

Gerth, Hans H. 1969. "The Nazi Party: Its Leadership and Composition." In *Studies in Social Movements: A Social Psychological Perspective,* ed. Barry McLaughlin, 258–74. New York: Free Press.

Gerth, Hans, and C. Wright Mills. 1946. *From Max Weber: Essays in Sociology.* New York: Oxford University Press.

Glatzer, Wolfgang, Karl Otto Hondrich, Heinz-Herbert Noll, Karin Stiehr, and Barbara Wörndl. 1992. *Recent Social Trends in West Germany, 1960–1990.* Frankfurt: Campus Verlag.

Glunk, Fritz R. 1996. *Der gemittelte Deutsche: Eine statistische Spurensuche.* Munich: dtv.

Goldhagen, Daniel. 1996. *Hitler's Willing Executioners: Ordinary Germans and the Holocaust.* New York: Knopf.

Goldthorpe, John H. 1985. "Soziale Mobilität und Klassenbildung. Zur Erneuerung einer Tradition soziologischer Forschung." In *Die Analyse sozialer Ungleichheit: Kontinuität, Erneuerung, Innovation,* eds. Hermann Strasser and John H. Goldthorpe, 174–204. Opladen: Westdeutscher Verlag.

———. 1987. *Social Mobility and Class Structure in Modern Britain.* Oxford: Claredon Press.

Gordon, Milton M. 1964. *Assimilation in American Life: The Role of Race, Religion and National Origins.* New York: Oxford University Press.

Habermas, Jurgen. 1984. *Reason and the Rationalization of Society.* Boston: Beacon Press.

Habich, Roland, Heinz-Herbert Noll, and Wolfgang Zapf. 1994. "Soziale Schichtung und soziale Lagen." In Statistisches Bundesamt, ed. *Datenreport.* 574–81. Bonn: Bundeszentrale für politische Bildung.

Habich, Roland, and Peter Krause. 1994. "Berufliche und soziale Mobilität von Ausländern." In Statistisches Bundesamt, ed. *Datenreport,* 589–607. Bonn: Bundeszentrale für politische Bildung.

Haller, Max. 1987."Positional and Sectoral Differences in Income: The Federal Republic, France, and the United States." In *Comparative Studies of Social Struc-*

ture: Recent Research on France, the United States, and the Federal Republic of Germany, ed. Wolfgang Teckenberg, 172–90. Armonk, NY: M. E. Sharpe.

Haller, Max, Wolfgang König, Peter Krause, and Karin Kurz. 1985. "Patterns of Career Mobility and Structural Positions in Advanced Capitalist Societies: A Comparison of Men in Austria, France, and the United States." *American Sociological Review*, 50:579–602.

Hamilton, Alastair. 1971. *The Appeal of Facism*. New York: MacMillian.

Hampden-Turner, Charles, and Alfons Trompenaars. 1993. *The Seven Cultures of Capitalism*. New York: Doubleday.

Hanesch, Walter, Wilhelm Adamy, Rudolf Martens, Doris Rentzsch, Ulrich Schneider, Ursula Schubert, and Martin Wisskirchen, eds. 1994. *Armut in Deutschland*. Reinbek: Rowohlt.

Hannan, Michael, Klaus Schomann, and Hans-Peter Blossfeld. 1990. "Sex and Sector Differences in the Dynamics of Wage Growth in the Federal Republic of Germany." *American Journal of Sociology* 55:694–713.

Harrison, Bennett, and Barry Bluestone. 1988. *The Great U-Turn: Corporate Restructuring and the Polarizing of America*. New York: Basic Books.

Hauser, Richard. 1995. "Das empirische Bild der Armut in der Bundesrepublik Deutschland ein Überblick." *Aus Politik und Zeitgeschichte* 31–32:3–13.

———. 1996. "Vergleichende Analyse der Einkommensverteilung und der Einkommensarmut in den alten und neuen Bundesländern 1990 bis 1995." Unpublished paper presented at the Hans Böckler Stiftung, Frankfurt/M.

Hauser, Richard, and Udo Neumann. 1992. "Armut in der Bundesrepublik Deutschland. Die sozialwissenschaftliche Thematisierung nach dem Zweiten Weltkrieg." In *Armut im modernen Wohlfahrtsstaat*, eds. Stefan Leibfried and Werner Voges, 237–71. Opladen: Westdeutscher Verlag.

Hauser, Richard, and Werner Hübinger. 1993. *Arme unter uns. Part 1: Ergebnisse und Konsequenzen der Caritas-Armutsuntersuchung*. Freiburg i. Brsg.: Lambertus Verlag.

Hegi, Ursula. 1997. *Tearing the Silence: On Being German in America*. New York: Simon and Schuster.

Henkel, Dieter. 1992. *Arbeitslosigkeit und Alkoholismus: Epidemiologische, ätiologische und diagnostische Zusammenhänge*. Weinheim: Beltz.

Hennis, Wilhelm. 1997. "Totenrede des Perikles auf ein blühendes Land." *Frankfurter Allgemeine Zeitung*, September 27, 1997, p. 36.

Hess, Henner. 1989. "Tabak." In *Drogen und Drogenpolitik: ein Handbuch*, ed. Sebastian Scheerer et al. Frankfurt/M.: Campus.

Hettlage, Robert, and Karl Lenz eds. 1995. *Deutschland nach der Wende. Eine Zwischenbilanz*. Munich: Beck.

Hoffmann-Lange, Ursula. 1992. *Eliten, Macht und Konflikt in der Bundesrepublik*. Opladen: Westdeutscher Verlag.

Hoffmeister, Gerhart, and Frederic C. Tubach. 1992. *Germany: 2000 Years: From The Nazi Era to German Unification*. Vol. III. New York: Continuum.

Hofstede, Geert. 1991. *Cultures and Organization: Software of the Mind*. New York: McGraw-Hill.

Holtmann, Dieter, and Hermann Strasser. 1990. "Comparing Class Structures and Class Consciousness in Western Societies." In *Class Structure in Europe: New Findings from East-West Comparisons of Social Structure and Mobility,* ed. Max Haller, 3–23. Armonk, NY: M. E. Sharpe.

Horowitz, Irving Louis. 1983. *C. Wright Mills: An American Utopian.* NY: Free Press.

Hraba, Joseph. 1994. *American Ethnicity.* Itasca, IL.: Peacock.

Hradil, Stefan. 1987. *Sozialstrukturanalyse in einer fortgeschrittenen Gesellschaft.* Opladen: Leske+Budrich.

———. 1992. "Die objektive und die subjektive Modernisierung: Der Wandel der westdeutschen Sozialstruktur und die Wiedervereinigung." *Aus Politik und Zeitgeschichte* No. 29–30:3–14.

———. 1995. "Die Sozialstruktur Deutschlands im europäischen und internationalen Vergleich." In *Gesellschaftlicher Wandel in Deutschland,* 6th ed. Ed. Bernhard Schäfers, 286–321. Stuttgart: Enke.

Inglehart, Ronald. 1989. *Cultural Change.* Princeton, NJ: Princeton University Press.

———. 1996. *Modernization and Postmodernization: Cultural, Economic, and Political Change in Forty-Three Societies.* Princeton, NJ: Princeton University Press.

Institut der Deutschen Wirtschaft, ed. 1998. *Zahlen zur wirtschaftlichen Entwicklung 1998.* Cologne: IW.

Ishida, Hiroshi, John H. Goldthorpe, and Robert Erikson. 1991. "Intergenerational Class Mobility in Postwar Japan." *American Journal of Sociology* 96:954–93.

Ismayr, Wolfgang, ed. 1997. *Die politischen Systeme Westeuropas.* Opladen: Leske Verlag+Budrich.

Jaschke, Hans-Gerd. 1994. *Rechtsextremismus und Fremdenfeindlichkeit: Begriffe, Positionen, Praxisfelder.* Opladen: Westdeutscher Verlag.

Johnson, Chalmers. 1982. *MITI and the Japanese Miracle.* Stanford: Stanford University Press.

Jones, A.H.M. 1974. *The Roman Economy.* Oxford: Basel Blackwell.

Kaelble, Hartmut. 1979. *Historische Mobilitätsforschung: Westeuropa und U.S.A. im 19. und 20. Jahrhundert.* Darmstadt: Wissenschaftliche Buchgesellschaft.

Kaiser, Andrea. 1996. *Was erreicht die deutsche Drogenpolitik? Eine ökonomische Analyse des illegalen Drogenmarktes.* Marburg: Metropolis-Verlag.

Kantzenbach, Friedrich Wilhelm. 1975. "Christentum in der Gesellschaft." Vol. 2. *Reformation und Neuzeit.* Hamburg: Siebenstern.

Kappelhoff, Peter, and Wolfgang Teckenberg. 1987. "Intergenerational and Career Mobility in the Federal Republic and the United States." In *Comparative Studies of Social Structure: Recent Research on France, the United States, and the Federal Republic of Germany,* ed. Wolfgang Teckenberg, 3–52. Armonk, NY: M. E. Sharpe.

Kaufmann, Felix-Xaver. 1975. "Familiäre Konflikte und gesellschaftliche Spannungsfelder." In Der Mensch in den Konfliktfeldern der Gegenwart, 165–88. Düsseldorf: Landeszentrale für politische Bildung.

————. 1989. *Religion und Modernität. Sozialwissenschaftliche Perspektiven*. Tübingen: Mohr.

Kennedy, Paul. 1987. *The Rise and Fall of the Great Powers: Economic Change and Military Conflict From 1500 to 2000*. New York: Random House.

Kerbo, Harold R. 1982. "Movements of 'Crisis' and Movements of 'Affluence': A Critique of Deprivation and Resource Mobilization Theories." *Journal of Conflict Resolution* 26:645–63.

————. 1996. *Social Stratification and Inequality: Class Conflict in Historical and Comparative Perspective*. 3rd ed. New York: McGraw-Hill.

Kerbo, Harold R., and John McKinstry. 1995. *Who Rules Japan?: The Inner Circles of Economic and Political Power*. Westport, CT: Greenwood/Praeger.

————. 1998. *Modern Japan: A Volume in the Comparative Societies Series*. New York: McGraw-Hill.

Kerbo, Harold R., and Richard A. Shaffer. 1992. "Lower Class Insurgency and the Political Process: The Response of the U.S. Unemployed, 1890–1940." *Social Problems* 39:139–54.

Kerbo, Harold R., Elke Wittenhagen, and Keiko Nakao. 1994a. *Japanische Unternehmen in Deutschland: Unternehmens struktur und Arbeitsverhältnis*. Gelsenkirchen: Veröffentlichungsliste des Instituts Arbeit und Technik.

————. 1994b. "Japanese Transplant Corporations, Foreign Employees, and the German Economy: A Comparative Analysis of Germany and the United States." Duisburger Beiträge zur Soziologischen Forschung.

Kiesewetter, Hubert. 1996. *Das einzigartige Europa: Zufuällige und notwendige Faktoren der Industrialisierung*. Göttingen: Vandenhoeck & Ruprecht.

Klemm, Klaus et al., 1992. *Bildungsplanung in den neuen Bundesländern. Entwicklungstrends, Perspektiven und Vergleiche*. Weinheim/Basel: Beltz.

Kocka, Jurgen. 1996. "Crisis of Unification: How Germany Changes." In *In Search of Germany*, eds. Michael Mertes, Steven Muller, and Heinrich August Winkler, 191–210. New Brunswick, NJ: Transaction Books.

Koester, Ludwig. 1997. "Warum die Reichen immer reicher werden. Von einer Gleichverteilung kann in Deutschland keine Rede sein." *Das Parlament* 33–34:2.

Koenig, Wolfgang. 1987. "Employment and Career Mobility of Women in France and the Federal Republic." In *Comparative Studies of Social Structure: Recent Research on France, the United States, and the Federal Republic of Germany*, ed. Wolfgang Teckenberg, 53–85. Armonk, NY: M. E. Sharpe.

Krockow, Christian Graf von. 1998. *Der deutsche Niedergang. Ein Ausblick auf das 21. Jahrhundert*. Stuttgart: Deutsche Verlags-Anstalt.

Ladd, Everett Carl and Karlyn H. Bowman. 1998. *Attitudes Toward Economic Inequality*. Washington, DC: AEI Press.

Lauk, Kurt J. 1996. "Germany at the Crossroads: On the Efficiency of the German Economy." In *In Search of Germany*, eds. Michael Mertes, Steven Muller, and Heinrich August Winkler, 95–122. New Brunswick, NJ: Transaction Books.

Lenski, Gerhard, Jean Lenski, and Patrick D. Nolan. 1991. *Human Societies: An Introduction to Macrosociology*. 6th ed. New York: McGraw-Hill.

Liedtke, Rüdiger. 1994. *Wem gehört die Republik?* Frankurt: Eichborn.

Lincoln, James R., and Arne L. Kallenberg. 1990. *Culture, Control, and Commitment: A Study of Work Organization and Work Attitudes in the United States and Japan.* New York: Cambridge University Press.

Lincoln, James R., Harold Kerbo, and Elke Wittenhagen. 1995. "Japanese Companies in Germany: A Case Study in Cross-Cultural Management." *Journal of Industrial Relations.* Spring.

Lipset, Seymour Martin. 1979. *The First New Nation: the United States in Historical and Comparative Perspective.* New York: Basic Books.

———. 1996. *American Exceptionalism: A Double-Edged Sword.* New York: W.W. Norton.

Lipset, Seymour Martin, and Earl Raab. 1970. *The Politics of Unreason: Right-Wing Extremism in America, 1790–1970.* New York: Harper and Row.

Lueken, Verena. 1997. "Aerger im Paradies. Nach dem Streik—die Wiederentdeckung der Arbeiter." *Frankfurter Allgemeine Zeitung,* August 26, 1997.

McCarthy, John D., and Mayer N. Zald. 1977. "Resource Mobilization and Social Movements: A Partial Theory." *American Journal of Sociology,* 82:1212–41.

McLellan, David. 1973. *Karl Marx: His Life and Thought.* New York: Harper & Row.

McMulhall, Michael G. 1969. *The Dictionary of Statistics.* 4th ed. Detroit, MI: CRC.

Mann, Golo. 1992. *Deutsche Geschichte des 19. und 20. Jahrhunderts.* Frankfurt/M.: Fischer Taschenbuch.

Mann, Horace. 1891. "Report for 1849." In *Life and Works of Horace Mann.* Vol. IV: *Annual Reports of the Secretary of the Board of Education of Massachusetts for the Years 1845–1848; an Oration Delivered Before the Authorities of the City of Boston, July 4, 1842.* Boston, MA.: Lee and Shepard.

Markovits, Andrei S. 1986. *The Politics of the West German Trade Unions: Strategies of Class and Interest Representation in Growth and Crisis.* Cambridge: Cambridge University Press.

Mayntz, Renate. 1984. "The Higher Civil Service of the Federal Republic of Germany." In *The Higher Civil Service in Europe and Canada,* ed. Bruce Smith, 46–101. Washington, DC: The Brookings Institution.

Mertes, Michael. 1996. "Germany's Social and Political Culture: Change Through Consensus?" In *In Search of Germany,* eds. Michael Mertes, Steven Muller, and Heinrich August Winkler, 1–34. New Brunswick, NJ: Transaction Books.

Meyer, Thomas. 1996. "Familienformen im Wandel." In *Die Sozialstruktur Deutschlands,* 2nd ed., by Rainer Geissler, 306–32. Opladen: Westdeutscher Verlag.

Meys, Werner, and Faruk Sen. eds. 1986. *Zukunft in der Bundesrepublik oder Zukunft in der Türkei? Eine Bilanz der 25 jährigen Migration der Türken.* Frankfurt/M.: Dagyeli Verlag.

Miegel, Meinhard. 1985. *Die verkannte Revolution (I): Einkommen und Vermögen der privaten Haushalte.* Stuttgart: Kohlhammer.

Milgram, Stanley. 1974. *Obedience in Authority.* New York: Harper Colophon Books.

Mills, C. Wright. 1959. *The Sociological Imagination*. New York: Oxford University Press.

Mishel, Lawrence, and Jared Bernstein. 1993. *The State of Working America, 1992–1993*. Armonk, NY: M. E. Sharpe/Economic Policy Institute.

Moore, Barrington. 1966. *Social Origins of Dictatorship and Democracy: Lord and Peasant in the Making of the Modern World*. Boston: Beacon.

Morris, L. 1995. *Dangerous Classes: The Underclass and Social Citizenship*. New York: Routledge.

Mosley, Leonard. 1978. *Dulles*. New York: The Dial Press.

Muench, Paul. 1996. *Lebensformen in der frühen Neuzeit. 1150 bis 1800*. Ullstein-Buch, no. 35597. Frankfurt a. M.: Ullstein.

Muller, Steven. 1996. "Democracy in Germany." In *In Search of Germany*, eds. Michael Mertes, Steven Muller, Steveen Winkler, and Heinrich August Winkler, 35–58. New Brunswick, NJ: Transaction Books.

Muller, Walter, Paul Luttinger, Wolfgang Koenig, and Wolfgang Karle. 1990. "Class and Education in Industrial Nations." In *Class Structure in Europe: New Findings from East-West Comparisons of Social Structure and Mobility*, ed. Max Haller, 61–91. Armonk, NY: M. E. Sharpe.

Nenning, Günther. 1990. *Die Nation kommt wieder*. Zurich: Interfrom.

Neumann, Udo. 1995. "Die Armut der Caritas-Klienten im Vergleich mit der Armut unter der westdeutschen Bevölkerung." In: *Die Caritas-Armutsuntersuchung: Eine Bilanz*, eds. Werner Hübinger and Richard Hauser, 70–81. Freiburg/Brsg.: Lambertus Verlag.

Oberschall, Anthony. 1973. *Social Conflict and Social Movements*. Englewood Cliffs, NJ: Prentice Hall.

Offe, Claus. 1997. *Varieties of Transition: The East European and East German Experience*. Cambridge, MA: MIT Press.

Ogburn, William F. 1964. *Social Change*. New York: Viking Press.

Organization of Economic Cooperation and Development, 1998. http://www.oecd.org/puma/stats/govexp.htm.

Palen, J. John. 1981. *The Urban World*. New York: McGraw-Hill.

Parkes, Stuart. 1997. *Understanding Contemporary German*. London: Routledge.

Pittman, David Joshua, ed. 1967. *Alcoholism*. New York: Harper & Row.

Piven, Frances Fox, and Richard Cloward. 1971. *Regulating the Poor: The Functions of Public Welfare*. New York: Pantheon Books.

———. 1982. *The New Class War: Reagan's Attack on the Welfare State and Its Consequences*. New York: Pantheon.

Plato, Alexander von, and Almut Leh. 1997. "Ein unglaublicher Frühling": Erfahrene Geschichte im Nachkriegsdeutschland 1945–48. Bonn: Bundeszentrale für politische Bildung.

Pross, Helge. 1971. "Die Ehe ist stabiler als ihr Ruf." *Evangelische Kommentare*, 501–4.

Raff, Diether. 1988. *A History of Germany: From the Medieval Empire to the Present*. Hamburg: Berg.

Ragin, Charles, and David Zaret. 1983. "Theory and Method in Comparative Strategies." *Social Forces.* 61:731–754.

Rastetter, Daniela. 1996."Freizeit braucht freie Zeit. Oder: Wie Männer es schaffen, Frauen die (Frei-)Zeit zu stehlen." In *Freizeit in der Erlebnisgesellschaft. Amüsement zwischen Selbstverwirklichung und Kommerz,* ed. H. A. Harmann and R. Haubl, 45–66. Opladen: Westdeutscher Verlag.

Reich, Robert B. 1991. *The Work of Nations.* New York: Knopf.

Reulecke, Jürgen. 1985. *Geschichte der Urbanisierung in Deutschland.* Frankfurt/M.: Suhrkamp.

———. 1995. "Rheinland, Westfalen von den 1850er Jahren bis 1914: Der Aufbruch in die Moderne." In *Gesellschafts und Wirtschaftsgeschichte Rheinlands und Westfalens.* Stuttgart: Kohlhammer, 79–128.

Ritzer, George. 1993. *The MacDonaldization of Society.* Thousand Oaks, CA: Pine Forge Press.

———. 1995. *Expressing America: A Critique of the Global Credit Card Society.* Thousand Oaks, CA: Pine Forge Press.

Said, Edward. 1997. *Covering Islam: How the Media and the Experts Determine How We See the Rest of the World.* Rev. ed. New York: Vintage Books.

Santel, Bernhard. 1995. *Migration in und nach Europa: Erfahrungen, Strukturen, Politik.* Opladen: Leske+Budrich.

Schäfers, Bernhard. 1997. *Politischer Atlas Deutschland: Gesellschaft, Wirtschaft und Staat.* Bonn: Dietz.

———. 1995. *Gesellschaftlicher Wandel in Deutschland: Ein Studienbuch zur Sozialstruktur und Sozialgeschichte.* 6th ed. Stuttgart: Enke.

Schewe, Dieter. 1996. "Sozialpolitik in der Defensive." In *Sozialer Fortschritt,* ed. Gesellschaft für sozialen Fortschritt, vol. 10 (October):233–34.

Schmalz-Jacobsen, Cornelia, and Georg Hansen, eds. 1997. *Kleines Lexikon der ethnischen Minderheiten in Deutschland.* Munich: Beck.

Schmidtchen, Gerhard. 1997. *Wie weit ist der Weg nach Deutschland? Sozialpsychologie der Jugend in der postsozialistischen Welt.* Opladen: Leske+Budrich.

Schulze, Gerhard. 1995. *Die Erlebnisgesellschaft.* 2nd ed. Frankfurt/M.: Campus.

Schulze-Buschoff, Karin. 1995. *Familie und Erwerbsarbeit in der Bundesrepublik: Rückblick, Stand der Forschung und Design einer Lebensformentypologie,* ed. Wissenschaftszentrum Berlin für Sozialforschung. Vol. FS III 95–402. Berlin.

Schumacher, Harald. 1995. *Einwanderungsland BRD.* 3rd ed. Düsseldorf: Zebulon.

Schwarz, K. 1995. "Zur aktuellen Geburtenentwicklung in den alten und neuen Bundesländern." *Zeitschrift für Bevölkerungswissenschaft* 20:331–34.

Schweer, Thomas. 1997. "Entstehungs und Verlaufsformen von Alkoholkarrieren Arbeitsloser: Eine qualitative Studie." In *Schwer vermittelbar: Zur Theorie und Empirie der Langzeitarbeitslosigkeit,* ed. Gabriele Klein and Hermann Strasser, 221–48. Opladen: Westdeutscher Verlag.

Schweer, Thomas, and Hermann Strasser. 1994. *Cocas Fluch: Die gesellschaftliche Karriere des Kokains.* Opladen: Westdeutscher Verlag.

———. 1995. "Drogenmarkt Deutschland: Die Szene im Wandel." *Aus Politik und Zeitgeschichte* 9:3–12

Shapiro, Andrew L. 1992. *We're Number One: Where America Stands—and Falls—in the New World Order.* New York: Vintage Books.

Shell, ed. 1997. *Jugend 1997.* Opladen: Leske+Budrich.

Simkus, Albert, and Peter Robert. 1989. "Attitudes Toward Inequality Under a Kind of Socialism: Hungary, 1987." Paper presented at the meeting of the Research Committee on Social Stratification of the International Sociological Association, Stanford University, August.

Simmel, Georg. 1905 and 1955. *Conflict and the Web of Group Affiliations.* ed. Kurt H. Wolff and Reinhard Bendix. New York: Free Press

Skocpol, Theda. 1976. "Old Regime Legacies and Communist Revolutions in Russia and China." *Social Forces* 55:284–315.

———. 1979. *States and Social Revolutions: A Comparative Analysis of France, Russia, and China.* New York: Cambridge University Press.

Smeeding, Timothy M. 1991. "U.S. Poverty and Income Security Policy in a Cross National Perspective." Luxembourg Income Study, Working paper 70.

Smelser, Neil J. 1976. *Comparative Methods in the Social Sciences.* Englewood Cliffs, NJ: Prentice Hall.

Sontheimer, Kurt. 1973. *The Government and Politics of West Germany.* New York: Praeger.

Spellerberg, Annette. 1996. *Soziale Differenzierung durch Lebensstile.* Eine empirische Untersuchung.

Spohn, Willfried, and Y. Michal Bodemann. 1989. "Federal Republic of Germany." In *The Capitalist Class: An International Study,* eds. Tom Bottomore and Robert J. Brym, 73–108. New York: New York University Press.

Statistisches Bundesamt. 1997. *Statistisches Jahrbuch der Bundesrepublik Deutschland 1996.* Wiesbaden: Statistisches Bundesamt.

———, ed. 1995. *Datenreport 1994: Zahlen und Fakten über die Bundesrepublik Deutschland.* 2nd ed. Bonn: Bonn aktuell.

———, ed. 1996. *Datenreport 1996. Zahlen und Fakten über die Bundesrepublik Deutschland.* Bonn: Bundeszentrale für politische Bildung.

———, ed. 1997. *Datenreport. Zahlen und Fakten über die Bundesrepublik Deutschland.* Bonn: Bundeszentrale für politische Bildung.

Stempel, Martin. 1986. *Zwischen Koran und Grundgesetz. Religiöse Betätigung muslimischer Ausländer in der Bundesrepublik Deutschland.* Doctoral dissertation. Hamburg.

Strasser, Hermann. 1973. "Abbau sozialer Ungleichheit durch vermehrte Ausbildung? (I)" *IBE-Bulletin* (December):36–52.

———. 1974. "Abbau sozialer Ungleichheit durch vermehrte Ausbildung? (II)" *IBE-Bulletin* (March):23–36.

———. 1986. "Das Ideal der sozialen Gerechtigkeit im Lichte von Ungleichheitstheorien." In *Soziale Ungleichheit und Sozialpolitik: Legitimation, Wirkung, Programmatik,* eds. Jürgen Krüger and Herman Strasser, 43–64. Regensburg: Transfer Verlag.

———. 1988. "Klassenstrukturen und Klassentheorien: Neue Entwicklungstendenzen in westlichen Gesellschaften." *Oesterreichische Zeitschrift für Soziologie* 13:20–33.

————. 1993. "Status Inconsistency and the Rise of National Socialism." In *Change and Strain in Social Hierarchies: Theory and Method in the Study of Status Inconsistency,* eds. Robert W. Hodge and Hermann Strasser, 372–404. New Delhi, India: Ajanta Books International.

————. 1997a. "The German Debate over Multicultural Society: Climax or Test of Organized Capitalism?" *Canadian Journal of Sociology* 22 (2):243–58.

————. 1997b. "Langzeitarbeitslose zwischen diskontinuierlichen Erwerbsverläufen und sozialer Selektion." In *Schwer vermittelbar: Zur Theorie und Empirie der Langzeitarbeitslosigkeit,* eds. Gabriele Klein and Hermann Strasser, 9–39. Opladen: Westdeutscher Verlag.

————. 1998. "Schwer vermittelbar: Perspektiven der Langzeitarbeitslosigkeit." *Der Rotarier* No. 5:18-22.

Strasser, Hermann, and Dieter Boumans. 1996. "Wie ein Hauch aus dem Paradies." *Deutsche Polizei* No. 9:23–25, No. 10:16–20.

Strasser, Hermann, and Klaus Haack. 1985. *Probleme der Industriegesellschaft.* Stuttgart: Klett.

Strasser, Hermann, and Susan C. Randall. 1981. *An Introduction to Theories of Social Change.* London and Boston: Routledge & Kegan Paul.

Sustek, Herbert. 1995. "Das gesellschaftliche Verhältnis der Familie in der Bundesrepublik Deutschland." *Aus Politik und Zeitgeschichte* No. 52–53:16–23.

Teckenberg, Wolfgang. 1990. "The Stability of Occupational Structures, Social Mobility, and Interest Formation." In *Class Structure in Europe: New Findings from East-West Comparisons of Social Structure and Mobility,* ed. Max Haller, 24–60. Armonk, NY: M. E. Sharpe.

Terwey, Michael. 1987. "Class Position and Income Inequality: Comparing Results for the Federal Republic with Current U.S. Research." In *Comparative Studies of Social Structure: Recent Research on France, the United States, and the Federal Republic of Germany,* ed. Wolfgang Teckenberg, 119–71. Armonk, NY: M. E. Sharpe.

Thelen, Kathleen A. 1991. *Union of Parts: Labor Politics in Postwar Germany.* Ithaca, NY: Cornell University Press.

Thies, Jochen. 1996. "Observations on the Political Class in Germany." In *In Search of Germany,* eds. Michael Mertes, Steven Muller, and Heinrich August Winkler, 281–94. New Brunswick, NJ: Transaction Books.

Thomassen, Johannes. 1994. "Pendelbewegung im Bereich der Industrie und Handelskammer Krefeld im ersten Viertel des 20. Jahrhunderts." In *Städtische Bevölkerungsentwicklung in Deutschland im 19. Jahrhundert. Soziale und demographische Aspekte der Urbanisierung im internationalen Vergleich,* eds. H.G. Haupt and P. Marchalck, 117–42. St. Katharinen: Scripta Meraturae.

Thurow, Lester. 1991. *Head to Head: The Coming Economic Battle Between the United States, Japan, and Europe.* New York: Morrow.

Tibi, Bassam. 1996. *Im Schatten Allahs. Der Islam und die Menschenrechte.* Munich: Piper.

Turner, Henry Ashby. 1985. *German Big Business and the Rise of Hitler.* New York: Oxford University Press.

Turner, Jonathan H. 1997. *The Institutional Order: Economy, Kinship, Religion, Polity, Law, and Education.* New York: Longman.

Turner, Jonathan, and Royce Singleton, Jr. 1978. "A Theory of Ethnic Oppression: Toward a Reintegration of Cultural and Structural Concepts in Ethnic Relations Theory." *Social Forces,* 56:1001–18.

Turner, Lowell. 1991. *Democracy at Work: Changing World Markets and the Future of Labor Unions.* Ithaca, NY: Cornell University Press.

United Nations. 1997. *Report of the International Narcotics Control Board for 1997.* New York: United Nations Publications.

Unternehmerverband Ruhr-Niederrhein e.V. 1998. *Positionen 1998: Strukturveränderungen aktiv gestalten.* Duisburg: Unternehmerverband Ruhr-Niederrhein e.V.

Valentin, Friederike. 1994. *Scientology - der Griff nach Macht und Geld.* 3rd ed. Freiburg/Brsg.: Herder.

Verba, Sidney, et al. 1987. *Elites and the Idea of Equality.* Cambridge, MA.: Harvard University Press.

von Beyme, Klaus. 1984. "The Power Structure in the Federal Republic of Germany." In *Contemporary Germany: Politics and Culture,* ed. Charles Burdick, Hans-Adolf Jacobsen, and Winfried Kudszus, 77–106. Boulder, CO: Westview Press.

Wallerstein, Immanuel. 1974. *The Modern World-System.* New York: Academic Press.

———. 1980. *The Modern World-System II: Mercantilism and the Consolidation of the European World Economy, 1600–1750.* New York: Academic Press.

———. 1989. *The Modern World-System III: The Second Era of Great Expansion of the Capitalist World Economy, 1730–1840s.* New York: Academic Press.

Weber, Juergen ed. 1991. *Geschichte der Bundesrepublik Deutschland.* Vol. 4, *Die Bundesrepublik wird souveraen, 1950–1995.* 2nd ed. Paderborn: Schoeningh.

Weber, Marianne. 1975. *Max Weber: A Biography.* Translated by Harry Zohn. New York: John Wiley & Sons.

Weber, Max. 1947. *The Theory of Social and Economic Organization.* Translated by Talcott Parsons. New York: Free Press.

———. 1958. *The Protestant Ethic and the Spirit of Capitalism.* Translated by Talcott Parsons. New York: Free Press.

Wehler, Hans-Ulrich. 1995. *Deutsche Gesellschaftsgeschichte.* Vol. 3, *Von der "Deutschen Doppelrevolution" bis zum Beginn des Ersten Weltkrieges, 1849–1914.* Munich: Beck.

———. 1996. *Deutsche Gesellschaftsgeschichte.* Vol. 1, *Vom Feudalismus des Alten Reiches bis zur Defensiven Modernisierung des Reformära, 1700–1815.* 3rd ed. Munich: C.H. Beck.

Weick, S. 1995. "Familie." In Statistisches Bundesamt, *Datenreport 1994.* 2nd ed., 508–20. Bonn: Bonn aktuell.

Wells, H.G. 1971. *The Outline of History.* New York: Doubleday.

Wever, Kirsten. 1991. "Codetermination and Competitiveness: What German Employers Think." Paper presented at the Industrial Relations Research Association, Anaheim, California.

Williams, Kirk. 1984. "Economic Sources of Homicide: Re-estimating the Effects of Poverty and Inequality." *American Sociological Review* 49:283–89.

Winkler, Heinrich August. 1996. "Rebuilding of a Nation: The Germans Before and After Unification." In *In Search of Germany*, eds. Michael Mertes, Steven Muller, and Heinrich August Winkler, 59–78. New Brunswick, NJ: Transaction Books.

———. 1997. *Streitfragen der deutschen Geschichte. Essays zum 19. und 20. Jahrhundert.* Munich: Beck.

Winter, Rolf. 1995. *Little America: Die Amerikanisierung der Deutschen Republik.* Hamburg: Rassch and Röhring.

Wittfogel, Karl A. 1957. *Oriental Despotism: A Comparative Study of Total Power.* New Haven: Yale University Press.

Zelle, Carsten. 1998. "Soziale und liberale Wertorientierungen: Versuch einer situativen Erklärung der Unterschiede zwischen Ost- und Westdeutschen." *Aus Politik und Zeitgeschichte* 41–42:24–36.

INTERNET RESOURCES

General Information about Germany

www.bundesregierung.de/
Basic facts about Germany

userpage.chemie.fu-berlin.de/adressen/brd.html
Basic facts about Germany

www.Statistik-bund.de/basis/be_ueber.htm
www.Statistik-bund.de/
Information from the German Government Bureau of Statistics

www.state.gov/www/background_notes/germany_9803_bgn.html
Survey of important information about Germany

www.bawue.de/~hanacek/info/archive.htm
Archives on various German topics

www.hdg.de/index.en.html
Web site of Bonn's "House of History"

The German Economy

www.commerzbank.com/daten/deutsch/deutsch.htm
Basic facts about the German Economy

The German Political System

www.bundesregierung.de
Federal government homepage

www.bundestag.de
Bundestag homepage

www.policy.com/issuewk/98/0928
Information and notes on current German politics

Education in Germany

www.tulane.edu/~rouxbee/children/germany1.html
Information and notes on education in Germany

Social Stratification

www.crab.rutgers.edu/~wood/strat.html
Information and notes on social stratification in Germany

www.wotan.wiwi.uni-rostock.de/~somakro/sektion/ungl_sek.htm
Web site of the Section on Social Inequality and Social Structural Analysis of the German Sociological Association

Social Problems

www.ifs.univie.ac.at/~uncjin/uncjin.html
UN crime statistics for nations around the world

www.ifs.univie.ac.at/~uncjin/germany.html
Crime statistics for Germany in particular

Newspapers

www.berliner-morgenpost.de/bm/international/index.html
Berlin Newspaper (some stories in English)

www.iht.com
The International Herald Tribune (One of the best international newspapers in English)

Other

www.entry.de/english/
Directory of German Web Servers

NAME INDEX

Abdullah, Muhammed S., 83, 84, 85, 127n
Abegglen, James C., 43
Anweiler, Oskar, 88, 89
Ardagh, John, 5, 23, 54

Backes, Uwe, 104
Bärsch, Claus-Ekkehard, 20
Barz, Heiner, 83
Beck, Ulrich, 125n
Bellers, Anni, 4
Bellers, Juergen, 4
Bendix, Reinhard, 6, 14, 37
Bernstein, Jared, 55, 56, 94
Bertram, Hans, 71
Blau, Judith, 98
Blau, Peter, 98
Blossfeld, Hans-Peter, 60, 61, 62
Bluestone, Barry, 96, 121
Bodemann, Michael Y., 54, 62, 63
Bornschier, Volker, 119, 120, 122
Boumans, Dieter, 101, 102
Bowman, Karlyn H., 35
Broom, Leonard, 21, 22, 63, 64, 126n
Brunt, P. A., 10
Buerklin, Wilhelm, 65
Burgess, Ernest W., 109
Burkart, G., 73

Carroll, Glenn R., 61
Chirot, Daniel, 11,12, 17, 18, 22, 24, 120, 121
Clark, Kenneth, 10
Cloward, Richard, 16, 97
Collins, Randall, 49
Coser, Lewis A., 106, 125n
Craig, Gordon A., ix, 5, 6, 13, 59

Dahrendorf, Ralf, 32, 65, 89
Davies, Norman, 10
Davis, Nancy J., 61, 107
de Tocqueville, Alexis, 52

Dettling, Warnfried, 45
Dicke, Klaus, 106
Dietrich, William S., 17, 32, 65
Domhoff, G. William, 64
Dorbritz, J., 69, 71, 74
Drauschke, Petra, 73
Durkheim, Emile, 76, 83

Eisel, Stephan, 111, 113, 115
Erbsloeh, Barbara, 70
Erikson, Robert, 62

Fallows, James, 17
Faruk, Sen, 84
Featherman, David, 62
Fischer, Andreas, 89
Fuerstenberg, Friedrich, 46

Garten, Jeffrey E., 42
Gärtner, K., 69, 71, 74
Geiger, Theodor, 69
Geissler, Rainer, 45, 69, 70, 89, 95
Gerlach, Michael L., 43
Gerth, Hans, 20, 21, 54
Glatzer, Wolfgang, 55, 59, 60, 61
Glunk, Fritz R., 127n
Goldhagen, Daniel, 18
Goldthorpe, John H., 62

Haack, Klaus, 68
Habermas, Jürgen, 65
Hamilton, Alastair, 21
Hampden-Turner, Charles, 6, 117
Hanesch, Walter, 55, 93, 95
Hannan, Michael, 60, 61
Hansen, Georg, 2
Harrison, Bennett, 96, 121
Hauser, Richard, 73
Hauser, Robert, 62
Hegi, Ursula, ix
Hettlage, Robert, 46

Hoffmeister, Gerhart, 23, 54, 57,
        61, 107
Hofstede, Geert, 6–7
Holtmann, Dieter, 60
Hraba, Joseph, 9
Hradil, Stefan, 74

Inglehart, Ronald, 70
Ishida, Hiroshi, 62
Ismayr, Wolfgang, 124n

Jaschke, Hans-Gerd, 104
Johnson, Chalmers, 17
Jones, A. H. M., 10

Kaiser, Andrea, 103
Kalleberg, Arne L., 49
Kappelhoff, Peter, 62
Kantzenbach, Friedrich Wilhelm, 79
Kaufmann, Felix-Xaver, 69, 77
Kennedy, Paul, 11, 13, 17, 18, 25,
        37, 121
Kerbo, Harold R., 7, 14, 17, 25, 32,
        36, 42, 43, 50, 53, 54, 56,
        57, 59, 61, 63, 64, 96, 97,
        121, 125n, 127n
Kiesewetter, Hubert, 14
Kocka, Jürgen, 113, 114, 116
Koenig, Wolfgang, 61
Krockow, Christian Graf von, 112

Ladd, Everett Carll, 35
Lenski, Gerhard, 67, 86
Lenski, Jean, 67, 86
Lenz, Karl, 46
Liedtke, Rüdiger, 43
Lincoln, James R., 49, 57
Lipset, Seymour Martin, 20, 35

McCarthy, John D., 25
McKinstry, John, 17, 32, 43, 54, 63, 64
McMulhall, Michael G., 14
Mann, Golo, 31
Mayer, Karl Ulrich, 61
McLellan, David, 16
Mertes, Michael, 34, 96, 108

Meyer, Thomas, 71, 72, 73
Meys, Werner, 84
Mills, C. Wright, 54, 92
Mishel, Lawrence, 55, 56, 94
Moore, Barrington, 14, 19, 24, 37
Mosley, Leonard, 23
Muench, Paul, 79
Muller, Steven, 118

Nakao, Keiko, 7, 50, 57, 127n
Nenning, Günther, 123
Neumann, Udo, 93
Nolan, Patrick D., 67, 86

Oberschall, Anthony, 20, 21
Offe, Claus, 118
Ogburn, William F., 114

Palen, J. John, 109
Parkes, Stuart, 60, 93, 104, 105, 106,
        108, 116, 118
Pittman, David Joshua, 103
Piven, Frances Fox, 16, 97
Pross, Helge, 69

Raab, Earl, 20
Raff, Diether, 6, 10, 13, 14, 18, 19, 76
Randall, Susan C., 69
Reich, Robert B., 121, 123
Robert, Peter, 36
Robinson, Robert V., 61, 107

Santel, Bernhard, 74
Schäfers, Bernhard, 68, 70, 71
Schewe, Dieter, 46
Schmalz-Jacobsen, Cornelia, 2
Schmidtchen, Gerhard, 104
Schomann, Klaus, 60, 61
Schulze, Gerhard, 73
Schulze-Buschoff, Karin, 70, 72
Schwarz, K., 72
Schweer, Thomas, 103
Shapiro, Andrew L., 42, 63, 78, 94,
        98, 99
Shay, William L., Jr., 21, 22, 63,
        64, 126n

Simkus, Albert, 36
Simmel, Georg, 106, 125n
Skocpol, Theda, 24
Smeeding, Timothy M., 93
Sontheimer, Kurt, 33
Spohn, Willfried, 54, 62, 63
Stalk, George, Jr., 43
Stolzenberg, Margit, 73
Strasser, Hermann, 19, 21, 39, 60, 68,
          69, 91, 93, 96, 101, 102, 105,
          127n, 128n
Sustek, Herbert, 73

Teckenberg, Wolfgang, 62
Thelen, Kathleen A., 48, 49, 57, 58,
          123, 125n
Thies, Jochen, 65
Thurow, Lester, 17, 41, 42, 119,
          121, 123
Tibi, Bassam, 127n
Trompenaars, Alfons, 6, 117
Tubach, Frederic C., 23, 54, 57, 61, 107
Turner, Henry Ashby, 21, 22, 57
Turner, Jonathan H., 77
Turner, Lowell, 48, 123

Valentin, Friederike, 85
Verba, Sidney, 91
von Beyme, Klaus, 54

Wallerstein, Immanuel, 12, 24, 120
Weber, Marianne, 19
Weber, Max, 7, 12, 24, 79
Wehler, Hans Ulrich, 14
Weick, S., 75
Wells, H.G., 10
Wever, Kirsten, 50, 123
Williams, Kirk, 98
Winkler, Heinrich August, 114, 118
Winter, Rolf, 27
Wittenhagen, Elke, 7, 50, 57, 127n
Wittfogel, Karl A., 11

Zald, Mayer N., 25
Zelle, Carsten, 4–5

SUBJECT INDEX

Adenauer, Konrad, 23, 33
aging, 107–108
AIDS, 100
amakudari in Japan, 65
Auschwitz, 21

bank Keiretsu, 43
Basic Law (Grundgesetz), 23,
    29–32, 113
Beamte (civil servants/bureaucrats),
    32, 65
Berlin Wall, 1, 23–25, 31, 111–113
Bismarck, Otto von, 16–17, 80
Bosch, Carl, 21
Bosch, Robert, 64
Brandt, Willy, 33, 57
Bundesrat, 31
Bundestag, 30–31, 65

Calvinism, 12
capitalism, 41–43
capitalist development state, 17
Chancellor, 30
China, early development, 11
Christian Democratic Union, 30, 33
class, definition of, 54
codetermination law(s), 48, 56–58
Cold War, 22–23, 24–25, 28, 120–121
collectivistic value system, 6
colonial empires, 17–18
communism, 41
    fall of, 111–113
Communist Party (SED), 33
corporations
    Japanese and German, 7
    stock control, 42–43, 66
crime and vice, 98–103
    international comparisons, 98–99
crude birth rate, 107
culture, 4
culture lag, 114–115
Czechoslovakia, 25

demography, 107
drug abuse, 101–103
dual labor representation system,
    48, 57
Durkheim, Emile, 76, 99, 100

East Germany
    Communist Party (SED), 33–34
    economic development, 45–46
    education in, 88–89, 90–91
    fall of, 111–113
    family system, 73
    German Democratic Republic
        (GDR), 24–25
    migration from, 23, 28, 111–113
    and religion, 81
    Soviet dominance of, 22–23, 24–25
    value orientations, 4–5
economic development, 44–46
economic miracle, 1, 22–24
education
    in Germany, 87–88
    history of, 86–87
    opportunities for, 89–91
*Elementary Forms of the Religious Life,
    The*, 76
Enlightenment Age, 13
Erhard, Ludwig, 23
ethnic minorities, 2
ethnocentrism, 5
European Central Bank, 119
European Commission, 39, 119
European Court, 39
European Parliament, 39, 119
European unification, 39–40, 117–119
European Union (EU), 35, 39–40,
    118–120

family
    changes in, 70–71
    in comparative perspective, 73–74
    demography of, 71–73

family—*cont.*
   divorce rates, 71–72, 107
   evolution of, 67
   extended, 68
   in Germany before WWII, 68–69
   as an institution, 67
   nuclear, 67–68
   patriarchical, 68
   in post war Germany, 68
Farben, I.G., 21
Federal President, 31
Federal Republic of Germany (West
      Germany), 28, 29
federal system, 31
federalism, 37
fertility rate, 72
feudalism, 10–11
   European, 10–11
Fischer, Joschka (Josef), 34
forced industrialization, 24
foreigners, 2
Franco–Prussian War of 1870–1871, 16
Frederick the Great, 13, 64
Free Democratic Party, 30, 33

Garibaldi, Giuseppe, 16
geography, 2
gender
   inequalities, 58–61
   role separation, 59
German
   aging, 107–108
   banks, 43
   Basic Law (Grundgesetz), 23,
      29–32, 113
   Beamte (civil servants/
      bureaucrats), 32
   birth rate decline, 107–108
   Bundesrat, 31
   Bundeswehr (military), 34
   capitalism, 42–43
   Chancellor, 29–30
   Christian Democratic Union,
      30, 33
   citizenship laws, 105–106
   closing laws, 47
   codetermination laws, 48, 56,
   corporate stock ownership,
      42–43, 66

German—*cont.*
   crime and vice, 98–103
   Customs Union, 15
   cuts in social programs, 38–39
   democratic institutions, 29–32
   disunity and late development,
      12–14
   divorce rates, 71–72, 107
   drug abuse, 101–103
   dual labor representation
      system, 48
   economic collapse, 1920s, 19–20
   economic development, 17, 42,
      44–46
   economic miracle, 1, 22–24
   economic recovery, post–War,
      22–24
   economic unification, 115–117
   education in, 86–88, 89–91
   elite unity, 64
   equalization of burdens law
      (Lastenausgleichgesetz), 54
   and European Union (EU),
      119–120
   family
      changes in, 70–71
      demography of, 71–73
      in East Germany, 73
      post war, 69–70
      before WW II, 69
   Federal President, 31
   federal system, 31
   fertility rate, 72
   Free Democratic Party, 30, 33–34
   gender
      inequality, 58–61
         international comparisons, 60
      role separation, 59
   "golden twenties," 20
   government ministry, 32
   Green Party, 29, 33–34, 122
   health care system, 38
   health insurance, 38
   hours employed, 46–47
   immigrants to the U.S., 9
   immigration, 105–106
   inequality, reduction of, 54–56
   judicial branch, 31
   labor laws, 56–58, 116
      history of, 56–58

German—*cont.*
  Laender (states), 31
  marriage rates, 107
  neo–Nazis, 104–105
  Partei des Demokratischen
      Sozialismus (PDS), 33–34
  political parties, 32–34
  political system, 28–32
  political unification, 113
  population problems, 106–108
  poverty level, 55, 93–98
  prostitution, 100
  Prussian values, 5–8
  psychological unification, 114–115
  racism and discrimination,
      103–106
  "red–green" alliance, 29, 122
  religion in, 77–78
    history of, 78–81
    today, 81–85
  rules/laws, 5
  sexual offenses, 100
  Social Democratic Party, 29, 31,
      33–34, 122
  social disorder, 5
  social security system, 108
  unemployment, 38–39, 93–98,
      104–105
  unemployment insurance, 38
  unification, 113–117
  unification, first, 14–16
  unions, 50, 56–58
  upper class, 63–66
  urban problems, 108–109
  values, 3, 5–8
  wages, 47–48, 56
    compared to other industrial
      nations, 56, 97
  war destruction, 44, 117
  welfare state, 34–39
  worker influence, 46–50, 56–58
  Works Constitution Act, 56–58
  works council, 48, 57–58
German Democratic Republic (GDR),
    24–25, 31
Germany
  early history, 10–11
  and World War I, 17–18
  and World War II, 18

Gini coefficient, Germany, 55
Green Party, 29, 33–34
Gorbachev, Mikhail, 25, 45, 111
government, attitudes toward, 36–37
government ministry, 32
grandes ecoles in France, 65

Haniel family, 64
health care, 38
Hitler, Adolf, 5–6, 18, 20
  and the church, 80–81
  and education, 87
  Hitler–Putsch, 20
  Mein Kampf, 20
  supporters, 20–22, 64
Hindenburg, President, 20, 31
Holocaust, 9
Holy Roman Empire, 10–11
Honecker, Erich, 28
Human Development Index, 59–60
Hungary, 25
hydraulic empires, 11

immigration, 105–106
income inequality, changes during
    1930s, 22
individualism, 6, 37
individualistic value system, 6
industrialization, 14
  forced, 24
inequality
  gender, 58–61
  reduced in Germany, 54–56
institutions, 27

Jews, attacks on, 20
judicial branch, 31
Junker class, 14, 19, 37

Kohl, Helmut, Chancellor, 29, 30, 31,
    33, 85, 122
Krupp, 21, 64

Laender (states), 31
List, Friedrich, 15

Little America: Die Amerikanisierung der Deutschen Republik, 27
Luther, Martin, 13, 76, 79
Maastricht Treaty, 118
MacArthur, George, General, 29
Marshall, George C., 23
Marshall Plan, 23, 44
Marx, Karl, 16
Meiji Restoration in Japan, 19
Mills, C. Wright, 92
modern world system, 12–14, 17–18, 120–122
moral economy, 37

National Socialism, 6
    and religion, 80–81
    rise of, 18–22
    supporters, 20–22
Nazi Party, 18–22
NATO (North Atlantic Treaty Organization), 33, 34
neo–Nazis, 104–105

parliamentary system, 30
Party of Democratic Socialism, 33–34
Poland, 25
political parties, 32–34
political violence, 25
population, 2
population problems, 106–108
poverty
    German rates, 55, 93–98
    international comparisons, 94
    versus unemployment, 96
    U.S. and Germany compared, 55
power/party, definition of, 54
Protestant Ethic and the Spirit of Capitalism, The, 12, 79
Protestant Reformation, 13, 79–80
protestantism and economic development, 12
Prusso–Austrian War of 1866, 16

racism, 5, 103–106
    international comparisons, 104
Reform Edict of 1807, 14
religion
    in Germany, 77–78

religion—*cont.*
    in Germany today, 81–85
    history of in Germany, 78–81
    international comparisons, 78
    Islam in Germany, 83–85
    sects, 78, 85
Reichstag, 20
Revolts of 1848, 15–16
revolution, 25
"Rhenish economy," 97
Roman Empire, 10
rules/laws, 5
Russian Revolution, 24

Schroeder, Gerhard, Chancellor, 29, 31, 33, 115, 122
Scientology, 85–86
sects, 78, 85–86
sexual offenses, 100
Siemens, 21
Siemens, Hermann Werner von, 21
Social Democratic Party, 29, 33
social disorder, 5
social mobility, 61–63
social movements, 25
social problems, definition of, 92
social security system, 108
social stratification
    definition, 53
    dimension of, 54, 58
    U.S. and Germany compared, 52–53
social structure, 4
Soviet Union
    collapse of, 24–25, 111–113
    dominance of East Europe, 22–25
status
    definition of, 54
    importance in Germany, 53
status attainment, 61–63
strikes, 50
suburbanization, 108

Taisho Democracy in Japan, 19
Thirty Years War, 13, 18
Thyssen, 21
Thyssen, Fritz, 21
Treaty of Versailles, 19
Treaty of Westphalia, 18

Treuhand, 116
Turks, 2, 83–85, 105–106
uncertainty avoidance, 7
unemployment, 38–39, 93–98
    international comparisons, 95, 97
    versus poverty, 98
unions, 50, 56–58
    industrial nations compared, 57
universities and the upper class, 65
upper class in Germany, 63–66
    definition, 63
    and industrial expansion, 64
    international comparisons, 63–64
    unity, 64–66
urban problems, 108–109

value orientations, 4
values, 3
von Humboldt, Wilhelm, 76

Walesa, Lech, 25
Wagner, Richard, 16
Weber, Max, 19, 79
Weimar Republic, 19, 31, 33
welfare development, 16
welfare state, 34–39
West
    and industrialization, 11
    and the world system, 11
William I, King of Prussia, 16
works councils, 48

zaibatsu, in Japan, 63